UP-FRONT REMODELING

Avoid the Home Remodeling Letdown by Knowing All Details and Costs *Before* Construction

Stephen Gidus

Building Harmony and Win-Win Relationships
Between Homeowners and Remodelers

Up-Front Remodeling
Avoid the Home Remodeling Letdown by Knowing All Details and Costs *Before* Construction

Author
Stephen Gidus

Copyeditor
Theresa Doerfler

Book & Cover Design
Paddy Morrissey

©2011 Stephen Gidus

ALL RIGHTS RESERVED. No part of this work covered by the copyright herein may be reproduced, transmitted, or stored, or used in any form by any means, graphic, electronic, or mechanical, including but not limited to photocopying, recording, scanning, digitizing, taping, Web distribution, information networks, or information storage retrieval systems, except as permitted under Section 107 or 108 of the 1976 United States Copyright Act, without the prior written permission of the author.

ISBN: 978-1-59571-744-3
Library of Congress Control Number: 2011940107

Printed in the United States of America on recycled paper

Published by
Word Association Publishers
205 Fifth Avenue
Tarentum, Pennsylvania 15084

www.wordassociation.com
1.800.827.7903

For product information, assistance or permission to use material from this text or product, submit all requests and questions by email to admin@remodology.com. Visit us at www.REMODology.com for more remodeling services and learning opportunities including an online course and books to purchase.

This publication is designed to provide competent and reliable information regarding the subject matter covered. However, it is sold and given with the understanding that the author and REMODology are not engaged in rendering legal, financial, or other professional advice. The author and those involved in producing this publication specifically disclaim any liability that is incurred from the use or application of the contents of this book. REMODology shall not be liable for any special, consequential, or exemplary damages resulting, in whole or part, from the reader's use of, or reliance upon, this material.

Table of Contents

About the Author II
Acknowledgements III
Introduction V

Chapter 1
Avoid Doubling Your Budget During Construction 1
   1. The Municipal Bypass 1
   2. Homeowners Associations 3
   3. Hookers – Build as You Go 3
   4. Clueless – Gee, I didn't know that 4
   5. Product Variance 4
   6. Do-It-Yourselfers 4

Chapter 2
The Pitfalls of Bidding Work in Residential Remodeling Construction 7
   1. The Traditional Methods of Remodeling Design and Bidding 7
      a) The Architect-Driven Process 7
      b) The Remodeler-Driven Process 8
   2. Bidding: Comparing Commercial Construction to Residential Construction – and Why It Matters to You ... 9
      a) Commercial Construction Including Remodeling and Additions 10
      b) Residential Construction Including Remodeling and Additions 12
      c) Residential Remodeling Bid Scenario 14
      d) Competitive Pricing 15

Chapter 3
Building the Project Twice – Dispelling the Myth "We Didn't Know What Was Behind the Walls" 17
   Why Remodelers Do Not Spend Time Doing Investigative Surgery 18

Chapter 4
Who's Who - The Architect's Role in Your Remodel 19
   1. Architect 19
   2. Residential Designer 20
   3. Draftsman 20
   4. Creativity Versus Technical Knowledge 20
   5. Either/Or 21
   6. Critical Team Member 21

Chapter 5
Who's Who - The Interior Designer's Role in Your Remodel 23
   1. Interior Designer 23
   2. Interior Decorator 24
   3. Critical Team Member 25

Chapter 6
Why Choosing the Remodeler First Makes Sense 27
   The Remodeler Is the Conductor 27

Chapter 7
Choosing the Right Remodeler – Is the Chemistry Right? 33
   1. Finding the Right Remodeler 33
   2. Additional Clues to Finding the Right Remodeler .. 33

Chapter 8
Comparing the Cost for a Remodel/Addition to the Cost for New Home Construction 37
   1. Square Foot Cost Defined 37
   2. Additional Factors Impacting Remodels and Additions ... 39
   3. Costs to Stay or Relocate 44

Chapter 9
An Overview of The Conflict-Free Home Remodeling Process 45
   1. The Process at a Glance 45
   2. Win-Win - Everyone Benefits 47

Homeowner Success Stories 51

Glossary 53–58

Up-Front Remodeling

About the Author

In 1987 Stephen Gidus partnered with his brother Paul to start their own home remodeling company – PSG Construction in metropolitan Orlando, Florida. In the beginning they "wore the tool belt" and personally did much of the actual construction work. As their projects grew in size and became more plentiful they slowly started to subcontract parts of the work to various trades with whom they began to build professional relationships. Although Stephen's construction company has constructed numerous custom homes, the majority of their work continues to focus on remodeling and additions to existing single-family homes.

Stephen has consistently been involved with the National Association of Home Builders on a local, state, and national level. He is a past president of the Home Builders Association of Metro Orlando as well as a former chairman of its Remodelers Council. He currently serves as a board member for the Florida Home Builders Association and is a past Remodelers Council chair as well as past Remodeler of the Year recipient. Additionally, he currently serves as a board member for the National Association of Home Builders.

Stephen has participated in numerous panel discussions in order to help educate the public on the intricacies of remodeling their homes, has written dozens of articles for the *Orlando Sentinel,* and has been interviewed by countless consumer and trade periodicals throughout the United States.

In addition to numerous industry-related awards for their remodeling work, PSG Construction received over 15 first-place or grand awards from the Home Builder's Association of Metro Orlando Parade of Homes Remodelers Showcase over a 13-year period.

In a constant pursuit to increase his knowledge in the new home construction and remodeling industry, Stephen obtained the following certifications from the National Association of Home Builders: Certified Graduate Remodeler (CGR), Certified Graduate Builder (CGB), Certified Green Professional (CGP), and Certified Aging in Place Specialist (CAPS).

Acknowledgement

To the proofreaders who edited the early versions of this book: Anne van den Berg, Jean Timpel, Cindy LaVigne, Michael Abernethy, Dixie Goolsby, Sandi Friel, and Victoria Mandracken.

To the custom home builders and remodelers who acted as technical proofreaders, giving me sound professional advice and feedback: Paul Thompson, Florida Home Builders Association; Marion McGrath, Jonathan McGrath Construction; Richard Reynolds, R.G. Reynolds Homes, Inc.; Monarcha Marcet, Adventure in Building, Inc.

A special mention to the National Association of Home Builders, Florida Home Builders Association and Home Builders Association of Metro Orlando for offering the educational and networking opportunities that have allowed me to build my remodeling company and the foundation for REMODology and The Conflict-Free Home Remodeling Process.

To my literary agent and manager, Victoria Mandracken, who has taken the vision for REMODology and Conflict-Free Remodeling and helped make it reality.

To my wife Tara and two boys who have patiently waited for the launch of REMODology and the completion of this book.

God Bless and thanks to you all!

Stephen Gidus

Introduction

If you've decided to move forward with a remodel or addition to your home, you've chosen the right book. If you don't know if remodeling or adding to your home is the right move or is even feasible, you've chosen the right book.

In Chapters 1-8 of this book, you will learn how to avoid spending more than you can afford, understand why remodeling seems more expensive than new construction, discover why putting a project "out to bid" can be a set-up for failure, and finally, understand all of the professionals involved in a remodeling project and the hierarchy of who's who. Chapter 9 of this book introduces you to the Conflict-Free Home Remodeling Process as an answer to how to avoid the potential pitfalls of home remodeling and how to avoid getting letdown along the way.

A good part of adding to or remodeling your home takes place up front – or should take place up front – before the actual construction begins. Throughout this book we will illustrate why this is important and what steps to take to get there. We believe in building the project on paper first, and then actually, in the field. A mistake can easily be corrected on paper, in the planning stage, but that same mistake found during construction can be extremely expensive.

You are about to embark on investing what might be the largest amount of money you have ever invested in anything – except for the purchase of your home. The entire premise behind this book is: spending time researching, understanding, and preparing before you start construction on your remodeling project will lead to a greater return on your investment and a much more successful completion of your home remodel. You will know all the details and costs involved Up-Front by following the Conflict-Free Home Remodeling Process.

This book and the other materials at REMODology.com are designed to help you with all your remodeling projects and show you how to avoid conflicts that could result in you, your family, or your savings getting letdown while pursuing your dream.

Definitions

HOMEOWNER
An individual owning his or her single family home, townhome or condominium.

REMODELER
A professional remodeler adding onto single family homes, townhomes or condominiums and licensed in his state or municipality if required by law.

REMODEL & REMODELING, RENOVATE & RENOVATING
For purposes of simplifying terms, we use the term "Remodel," which can mean the following:
▶ To alter the existing structure.
▶ Whole House Remodel – renovation of every room or just about every room in the house with exterior modifications including new additional living or storage space.
▶ Addition – the addition of more living or storage space joined to the existing space.
▶ Interior Remodel – modifications to individual rooms in the home with or without changes to the floor plan layout or structure of the building.

Avoid Doubling Your Budget During Construction

One of the key themes in this book is illustrating to the homeowner how to determine most effectively the actual cost of the project prior to going to construction. So often, I hear of homeowners starting construction with a particular cost or budget in mind only to have the budget drastically exceeded or even doubled during construction. Several scenarios in which homeowners get caught with escalating prices during construction range from remodeler ignorance and forgetfulness to hiring an unscrupulous remodeler.

The Municipal Bypass – Discovering Governmental Regulations After the Fact

Government organizations that are related to the building industry are ever increasing. There are quite a number of government-related agencies that will have a say in what can or cannot be completed on a particular project. One of the biggest mistakes I see with the municipal bypass faux pas is the remodeler or homeowner not being aware that a particular government agency needs to be involved and not finding out until the project has begun. This can become heartbreaking because not only will the cost of the project increase, but the project will probably be delayed as well.

A "municipality" means any local governing body including but not limited to city, town, county, parish, or township. Let's look at some of these agencies and how they might affect you:

▶ Municipal Building Department

A building permit is required in many municipalities regardless of the scope of work (interior or exterior). If discovered during the construction period, the municipal building department may "red tag" the project and force the homeowner and remodeler to stop construction. Construction may resume only after the appropriate plans have been drawn and submitted to the building department for their review and approval.

▶ Zoning Department

Many homeowners and remodelers envision building an addition to an existing home wherever they please on a section of the homeowner's property. Most municipalities have zoning regulations which specifically outline imaginary boundaries called setbacks in which no structure may be built. Many zoning departments have restricted height limits as well as a maximum allowable percentage of coverage on any given piece of property. In other words, a certain percentage of the property may not be covered with any building, sidewalk or driveway and must be kept permeable in order for rainwater to naturally percolate through the soil.

Up-Front Remodeling

If you are considering a whole-house remodel where a substantial percentage of the home is being improved, and your geographic region is subject to the potential impact of flood, wind, or seismic conditions, you may be subjected to upgrading the entire home.

Substantial percentage is typically defined as touching or impacting more than a certain established square foot area percentage (such as 50% or more) of the existing home. In other cases it may be defined by the amount of money spent to improve the home versus the appraised value of the home. The formulas vary depending on the region and the governing body.

▶ Health Department

If your home utilizes a septic system, as opposed to city sewer for waste water disposal, the municipal health department may be involved. In the last five years, environmental agencies have made septic systems a notable target because of so many installed incorrectly or out of compliance to today's new standards. Regardless of whether you are adding on new space that does not include a bathroom, you still may be subject to a review by the health department.

Septic tank capacity is now determined by the square foot space of the entire house and not by the number of bathrooms. The health department is interested in the potential number of occupants dwelling in a structure, potentially impacting the size of the septic system, rather than the number of bathrooms.

▶ Water Management District

If your home is located on a lake, river, stream, or any other body of water, the regional water management district will be involved. Years ago, many homes were built too close to bodies of water and the interior finished floor level set too low in relationship to the potential high watermark of that body of water.

Many water management districts have redefined the minimum distance an addition can be built to that body of water. Additionally, because of flooding history, some water management districts have established new interior finished floor levels. This means a new addition may need to be one or two feet higher than the existing interior floor levels. In many cases, if an addition or remodel is impacting a certain percentage of the whole house (in some cases 50% or more) the water management district has the right to make the homeowner raise the level of the entire home so that all interior finished floor levels are at the new required finished floor elevation.

Can you imagine discovering that the entire house will need to be raised to meet a new minimum floor elevation, after your remodeler has already started demolition to the existing house? I've seen this happen and it can be devastating to the homeowner who does not have the financial resources to pay for the additional work – after it is too late to reconsider.

▶ Historic Preservation Board

Some homeowners and remodelers may not realize the home is located within a historic preservation district. Historic preservation boards have the authority to dictate to the homeowner and remodeler what the exterior of an addition or remodel may or may not look like. They also have the authority to dictate what types of materials may or may not be used on the exterior. If your home is located within a historic preservation district and you have not prepared for their review, submission and approval may add up to two or three months or more to the process.

▶ Utility Companies

At some point in the planning stage, research should take place to determine whether or not there are overhead or underground utilities requiring relocation due to the placement of a new structure. Neglecting to address existing utilities may cause a tremendous amount of delay during construction and will most certainly create additional cost.

The failure to identify and engage with the appropriate municipal departments at the right time can lead to months of delays and potentially tens of thousands of dollars of additional cost expended for a project. It is so important to understand the relationships these municipal departments have within your community, and more importantly, how they may or may not be required to be involved in the planning and execution of your project.

Homeowners and remodelers with little experience can very easily be caught in the municipal bypass if they are not savvy enough to understand what steps must be taken before construction.

Homeowners Associations

Similar to the municipal bypass and government regulations, homeowners associations will have a say about what you can and cannot do to the exterior of your property. If you live in a community with a homeowners' association and the remodel affects the exterior of the home, the association will usually want to approve a conceptual plan before approving a final plan. Homeowners' associations may also critique and approve exterior finishes such as windows, roofing materials and paint colors.

If you live in a condominium, the governing association will want to know what work will be taking place on the interior and be assured the remodeling will not impact a neighbor adjacent to the project location.

It is critical to begin dialogue with the homeowners' association during the initial steps of the Pre Construction phase.

Hookers – Build as You Go

Hookers are remodelers who usually know what needs to be done to accomplish the homeowner's desired scope of work but intentionally omit, eliminate, or "forget" to include all that is necessary to complete that scope of work. His initial estimate appears low and appealing compared to another remodeler's proposal that may consider and calculate all that is necessary to complete the desired scope of work.

The hooker's angle is to get the homeowner excited about his company because of the seemingly lower, more appealing budget. However, as soon as the homeowner is hooked and engaged (after the start of construction), the hooker then begins to "discover" items he "did not know about."

After the omitted, eliminated or "forgotten" work is discovered, the hooker proposes the additional cost to the homeowner. The homeowner has little choice but to pay for the additional work and move forward. In many cases, the total cost the homeowner ends up paying the hooker equals the initial proposed budget from a more reputable remodeler.

Up-Front Remodeling

Clueless – "Gee, I didn't know that."

This particular remodeler is a more honest version of the hooker. He may be very well intentioned; however, he is ignorant usually because he is in over his head and does not have the necessary experience.

This remodeler may be very experienced with interior remodels to existing space and is being asked to build an addition on the exterior of an existing home– something he may have very little experience with. Another example might be a remodeler working in a historic preservation district without any idea of how critical it is to match existing materials.

When a homeowner works with a clueless remodeler who has little or no experience with certain types of projects, he takes the risk of getting less-than-desired results or paying more money along the way to achieve the desired goal.

Product Variance

The product variance applies to allowance items. These variables in the initial planning and budgeting stages of the project are set as a benchmark from which to work. These products include but are not limited to plumbing fixtures, electrical fixtures, cabinets, and countertops, floor coverings, and appliances. In the initial planning stages, the remodeler will assign a particular value for each of these items or products, either based on the equivalent of the home's existing fixtures, or based on the homeowners' indication of their desired goals.

In many cases, in an effort to move the project along and get it from the planning stage into the construction stage, the project will move to the construction stage without identifying the actual final product selections.

A final agreement will be drafted and approved by the homeowner with the original allowance items identified along with the projected cost for each of those allowance items.

In some cases, the remodeler underestimates the homeowners' desired tastes, or the homeowners underestimate their own desired tastes – related to the actual cost of a particular product. This becomes apparent when the homeowners eventually begin to identify and select the allowance items either on their own or with the interior designer. If the homeowners select products at a more expensive cost than the remodeler calculated, the variance of cost for the project now increases. Not all homeowners are prepared for the additional cost.

A method to eliminate this challenge is to identify all of these items prior to the start of construction. The homeowners can then re-examine the entire project and either accept the fact that the budget has grown due to additional costs associated with the allowance items or decide to eliminate a portion of the scope of work.

Discovering cost overruns in the Pre Construction phase of planning a home remodel rather than during construction allows homeowners much greater latitude to make more appropriate decisions about how to handle such expenses.

Do-it-Yourselfer

Planning for and executing your own remodeling project is like a defendant representing himself at trial instead of hiring an attorney, or performing surgery on yourself or a loved one instead of hiring a surgeon. The outcome could be disappointing or disfiguring.

What many homeowners forget to consider when embarking on their own major remodeling project is this: what is my time worth?

I see many stay-at-home moms or dads, parents, or individuals with full-time careers trying to tackle one of these projects. The lives of the children and quality of life at home suffer because the caregiving parent is no longer around, mom's business begins to suffer because she has lost focus on her career and is spending her time meeting with the carpenter to discuss unfamiliar details of the project, or the dynamics of the family become stressed because dad is working outside of his realm and every failure throughout the project becomes magnified at the dinner table.

Most homeowners have no idea of the government agencies involved in a remodeling project or what questions to ask a trade* or supplier regarding what is or what is not included in his particular scope of work. Many homeowners have an unrealistic expectation of what the project will cost because they have forgotten, or don't know, to include key components necessary to complete the desired scope of work, only to find out along the way as the cost continues to skyrocket beyond their original expected budget.

In order to achieve peace of mind and a more harmonious family life during the course of planning and construction, a remodeler who focuses on spending detailed time planning prior to the start of construction can be the best person to guide you through your project.

*A "trade" is a company or individual (sometimes also referred to as a trade contractor, trade partner, construction trade or subcontractor) providing labor to build any part of a project. Trades may also, in some situations, act as the supplier as well. For example a drywall trade may supply the drywall boards, drywall tape, corner bead, drywall tape compound, and fasteners, as well as the necessary labor to install the drywall.

The Pitfalls of Bidding Work in Residential Remodeling Construction

The Traditional Methods of Remodeling Design and Bidding

Pitfall #1. The Architect-Driven Process

In the architect-driven process, the homeowner approaches the architect first and works with him or her to develop plans for the remodeling project.

When the architect is driving a remodeling process, an all-too-familiar scenario might look like this: The homeowners want to add a new 20' x 25' master bedroom, closet and bathroom, and convert the existing master bedroom and bathroom into a study.

The homeowner may or may not ask the architect's opinion of how much the architect thinks the addition may cost; however if the homeowner does ask, the architect's answer may be something like this, "Well, a new home costs X amount of dollars for X amount of square feet. Divide the total cost of the home by the amount of square feet and you get a cost per square foot for the new addition."

Up-Front Remodeling

The homeowner is satisfied with the architect's cost analysis and orders the architect to develop the plans for the addition. The architect designs and engineers a full set of construction drawings, contacts two remodelers he knows, and one remodeler whose name was given to him by the homeowner, and puts the project out for "bid" to the three remodelers.

All three remodelers, using their own systems and procedures, compile estimates for the cost of the project.

▶ Remodeler #1 visits the home when the homeowner is not present, walks the property to assess the project site, returns to his office, and completes his estimate.
▶ Remodeler #2 meets with the homeowner and reviews the home from the inside and outside, asks the homeowner various questions, and then returns to his office to complete his estimate.
▶ Remodeler #3 visits the homeowner at the project location and meets with some of his key trades. He, like Remodeler #2, asks the homeowner some specific questions about the finishes and scope of work. He then returns to his office to complete his proposal.

All three remodelers then submit their estimates to the architect and homeowner for review. The results are shocking. All three estimates are at least double what the architect calculated, and the three estimates are 10% to 50% different from one another.

The architect blames the remodelers for being overpriced. The remodelers blame the architect for not giving the homeowner a realistic expectation for what the project should cost. The homeowners are beside themselves, frustrated and upset, not knowing whom to believe – the architect or the remodeler, or neither. After spending thousands of dollars with the architect, the homeowner's dream of adding a new master bedroom to the home is abandoned.

The architect may have been well intentioned but he is an architect, not a builder or remodeler. Most architects do not spend much time with trades and suppliers, pricing and purchasing their services and products, so how would they be qualified to understand how much a remodel will cost? In residential construction, the architect's primary job is to conceptually create the homeowner's dream on paper and convey that to the homeowner and remodeler.

The remodelers may have been well intentioned too, but lack of details and product description leaves a great deal of ambiguity between the architect's plans and what the homeowner wants. Later in this chapter in the section "Residential Construction Including Remodeling and Additions" we will look at why each remodeler looks at a typical set of residential plans differently from another.

Pitfall #2. The Remodeler-Driven Process

In a typical remodeler-driven process, the homeowner approaches the remodeler first. If the remodeler offers in-house design-build services, he will develop the plans using his in-house design team. If the remodeler does not offer in-house design build services, he will probably refer the homeowner to an architect, residential designer, or draftsman or subcontract with one of the three.

The typical remodeler will drive the design process as quickly as possible for one main reason: to get the project into construction and start generating revenue. This certainly makes sense for the remodeler but there is an inherent drawback for the homeowner.

The estimating or bidding phase of the remodeler-driven process is typically done from the remodeler's office. Occasionally, to clarify some details, he will meet some of the trades or suppliers at the project site.

While the addition may be structurally sound, sacrifices are typically made in the areas of product selections, product type, and the matching of existing finishes and details within the existing home. In an effort to get the project into construction as quickly as possible, the remodeler may bypass the involvement of the homeowners and their opinion on these decisions and choices.

Generally speaking, I have found this oversight and sacrifice is typically not due to the greed or self-centeredness of the remodeler, but to one particular reason and that is, as Larry the Cable Guy puts it, to "Get'er done." Most remodelers are doers. They are action-takers; they want to see progress, immediate results, a finished product. So, in that vein, they take it upon themselves to make assumptions for the homeowner, thinking they know best.

The oversight and exclusion of homeowner participation is then discovered during the construction process. At this point, painful decisions need to be made by the homeowner. Typically, those decisions are followed by additional cost and construction time or sacrifices of not getting what the homeowner had originally envisioned prior to construction.

Pitfall #3: Bidding: Comparing Commercial Construction to Residential Construction – and Why It Matters to You

When we speak of bidding on a remodel or addition, we are really speaking of comparison shopping. For example, if I want to bid on or comparison shop for a new digital camera, I might begin by searching for what I want by either going to a retail store and physically examining the different brands and types of cameras, or searching the Internet until I find what I want to purchase. My next step would be to call several retail stores and ask them how much the certain camera (model name and number) sells for, or go online and search for companies who sell the same product. Based on the research and comparison of the product, I can make the decision of where to purchase the camera.

When we claim bidding does not work for residential remodeling, we first need to look at how bidding works in commercial construction.

Up-Front Remodeling

Commercial Construction

Commercial Construction, Including Remodeling and Additions

When the idea for a commercial addition or remodel project is conceived, the building owner hires an architectural firm to create a set of plans for the project. In most states, the architect is required to be licensed and registered with the state. The architect is the principal person for the design process. In addition the architect hires several consultants who assist in the building design.

Architect (Commercial Construction)

The architect's role is to design and create a space from an idea and put that vision on paper so it can be seen and understood by the individuals building it – eventually becoming a reality. There is a creative and a technical side to what the architect does. The space needs to be beautiful as well as functional. The architect acts as the owner's advocate in front of the municipal building and zoning departments, making sure all requirements are met. The architect in commercial construction is the orchestrator of the planning process.

Mechanical, Electrical, and Plumbing Engineer (Commercial Construction)

This engineer designs the mechanical, plumbing, and electrical systems.

Mechanical

The mechanical engineer designs and specifies the heating, air conditioning, and ventilating systems.
▶ Who is the manufacturer and what size is the heating and air conditioning system?
▶ What is the energy rating on the system?
▶ What size and type of ductwork will be used?
▶ What type of supply air diffusers will be used?
▶ What is the manufacturer and size of the bathroom and kitchen exhaust fans?

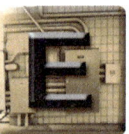

Electrical

The electrical engineer designs all areas of the project related to the electrical systems.
▶ What size and how many amperes of service will be required?
▶ What type of wire will be used?
▶ What type of switches and outlets will be used?
▶ How will the electrical system be grounded?
▶ What is the maximum number of lights or switches allowed to be used on each breaker?

Plumbing

The plumbing engineer designs and specifies the plumbing systems.
▶ What type and size of water supply lines will be used?
▶ What type and size of waste line will be used?
▶ Where and how will the new plumbing supply and waste lines tie into the existing lines?
▶ If the building is on a septic system, how will the new waste line be tied into the new or existing system?

Commercial Construction

Structural Engineer (Commercial Construction)
The structural engineer focuses on the structural elements in the addition or interior remodel. The structural elements include the foundation, roof trusses, and wall sections (how the walls will be constructed). The structural engineer also determines how the two buildings (when referring to an addition to an existing structure) will be structurally tied together and how existing interior structural walls will be modified if removed or altered.

Civil Engineer (Commercial Construction)
The civil engineer orders the survey for the property and gives the architect information about the layout and contour of the property. This information helps the architect determine where the new additions can be located and how the new buildings will be affected by the contour of the land. The civil engineer also designs the location of driveways and walks. If the building is on a septic system, the civil engineer determines what size the septic system will need to be and where it will be located.

Interior Designer (Commercial Construction)
The interior designer selects, identifies, and lists all of the finished products to be used in the building. Some examples of those products include the following:

- Plumbing fixtures
- Electrical fixtures
- Exterior doors
- Interior doors
- Cabinets
- Counter tops
- Tile flooring
- Carpet

Additional drawings are also provided by the interior designer and they may include:
- Elevations of the kitchen and bathroom walls, locating and defining all fixtures and equipment
- Closet systems and layouts
- Floor and wall tile layout
- Wood trim details, including baseboards, window and door casings, crown mouldings, and chair railings

Landscape Designer (Commercial Construction)
The landscape designer designs and specifies all items related to landscape and hardscape. Landscape is related to vegetation and hardscape is related to hard surfaces like walkways and planters. The landscape designer will design and specify the following:

- Plant materials and their locations
- Irrigation system
- Walkways
- Planters
- Privacy walls
- Retaining walls
- Fencing

Up-Front Remodeling

The architect takes all of this information and compiles it into two final documents:

1. Construction Drawings

The construction drawings, also called plans, are the combination of the architect's, engineer's, and designer's plans (the plans are the large pieces of paper measuring approximately 42" x 32" – sometimes bigger or smaller) from the above disciplines who have participated in developing the technical aspects of the project.

2. Specifications Manual

The specifications manual is a written outline and description of what is expected to be constructed. The specifications work in harmony with the plans. Here are a couple of examples:

a) The plans show the walls of the structure to be built with concrete block. The specifications indicate what type of block and mortar should be used to bond the block together and what type of reinforcing steel should be used, along with much more associated information.

b) The plans show the location of the windows and how the windows should be located in each opening. The specifications indicate the window manufacturer, the type of glass and screens to be used, along with other associated information pertaining to the windows.

What Does It Mean?

If an owner is trying to compare one builder to another solely based on price, this information is very meaningful and necessary in order to get an accurate comparison.

I once acted as the owner's agent for the addition of a 2400 square foot education building attached to an existing building. The project was a very simple rectangular building consisting of five classrooms, two storage rooms, a mechanical room, and two bathrooms. The plans, including the above components, consisted of 33 pages of detail and instruction. Additionally, a 200-page specification binder outlining every piece of mechanical equipment and product selection was developed. When we put the project out to bid, we were very confident each of the commercial builders looking at the project was looking at the same thing. All builders were competing equally - using the exact same information.

In commercial construction, with projects of this size, the goal in theory—and in most cases in reality–is for the design team to uncover and address every possible issue associated with that project. Additionally, the goal is to dot every "i" and cross every "t" upfront, before the project begins.

Residential Construction, Including Remodeling and Additions

In residential construction, the plans and specifications are typically much different from those of a commercial construction project. Comparing the same scale or type of project; at best you might get 8 to 10 pages of construction plans but probably 4 to 6 pages and in most cases no specifications manual. Why is this? What is different? Why does it matter? How does that impact you, the homeowner?

Let's look at the different professionals involved in the commercial project and compare to a residential project:

Residential Construction, Including Remodeling and Additions

Architect (Residential Construction)
The general plans for a remodel typically are much more vague and ambiguous than those for a commercial project. In the residential segment of remodeling, many details are left blank or are vague and left to the interpretation of the remodeler. Many of the details provided for the commercial builder are non-existent for the residential builder or remodeler.

Civil Engineer (Residential Construction)
The use of a civil engineer is almost always non-existent in residential construction. The architect or remodeler will order a survey of the property if he or she thinks it is necessary.

Structural Engineer (Residential Construction)
Municipalities that require a building permit typically require a structural engineer to certify the structural components of the addition or remodel. This process in residential construction is typically similar to commercial construction.

Landscape Designer (Residential Construction)
The use of a landscape designer is rare. The architect may give some indication of where the driveway or walks will go and whether a retaining wall or fence is needed. The remodeler will usually determine what materials and methods for installation will be used.

Mechanical, Electrical and Plumbing Engineer (Residential Construction)
In residential construction, these professional engineers are typically non-existent.

Mechanical
The heating, ventilating, and air conditioning trade usually specifies the type and size of equipment used, as well as the size of the air supply ducts. In some municipalities, energy calculations are required and this trade usually provides them.

Electrical
The electrician determines whether or not additional service is required for the new structure and if he or she thinks additional service is required, determines how many additional amperes are needed. The electrician also will determine where the interior service panel and exterior disconnect boxes will be located.

Plumbing
The plumbing trade typically specifies the type of supply and waste pipe used and determines how the systems will tie into one other.

Up-Front Remodeling

Interior Designer (Residential Construction)

Some homeowners and architects work with interior designers to help make product selections. If not, each remodeler will determine what products will be used and what allowance will be used until a final selection is made by the homeowner. Additional decisions such as window and door types, closets and trim materials type, and locations of these items are interpreted differently by each remodeler bidding on the project.

Specifications Manual (Residential Construction)

Most architects do not provide specifications; for those who do, a good bit of it is boilerplate.

Many of the decisions are left to the remodeler and his trades to determine and specify. The fact that the remodeler and trades are assisting in the decision making is not the issue or the challenge. *The challenge is when the homeowner or architect puts a residential project out to bid to three or four remodelers. The result will be three or four totally different prices because each remodeler is looking at the project and specifying items in different ways.*

One remodeler may be thinking, "What are the best products and methods I can use to make the new addition look as much like the original while using energy efficient products and best building practices?"

Another remodeler may be looking at the project thinking, "What building products and methods can I use to make my bid as low as possible so I can win this project? After all, the plans and specifications are vague and ambiguous so I'm really not cheating."

The end result is a homeowner who is confused by several bids he or she thought were derived from the same information but were obviously so different that one company interpreted something very differently from the other company.

Let's look at a Residential Remodeling Bid Scenario

A typical residential remodeling bid scenario is extremely different from a commercial construction project. In the majority of the cases as in this one, mechanical engineering, electrical engineering, plumbing riser plan, specifications and product selection are not identified. The architect submits the construction documents for "bid." Let us compare some bidding examples:

a) **HVAC System**
1) Remodeler A bids the mechanical system using a 3 ½ ton unit with a 16 SEER rating.
2) Remodeler B bids the mechanical system using a 3 ton unit with a 12 SEER rating.

b) **Electrical**
1) Remodeler A bids the electrical system using a 300 amp breaker panel with an underground power main from the power pole at the street.
2) Remodeler B bids the electrical system using a 200 amp breaker panel with an overhead power main from the power pole at the street.

c) Finish Trim Package
1) Remodeler A looks at the existing home and bids using solid-core pine, six-panel doors, 6-inch-high baseboard, 3½-inch casing and windows wrapped with wood jambs and casing.
2) Remodeler B bids using hollow core composite six-panel doors, 3½-inch high baseboard, 2½-inch casing and windows wrapped with drywall.

d) General Services
1) Remodeler A includes time to oversee product selection, time to manage a bid conference, more for weekly site cleaning and protection of the existing home…
2) Remodeler B does not.

This example compares just four areas for this particular project. Can you imagine the difference in cost between the two remodelers A and B after all of the items related to this project have been calculated? Remodeler A has made more costly assumptions so Remodeler B is going to look like he is the most cost-efficient remodeler looking out for the homeowner's best interest.

Competitive Pricing

If the question "How do I know I am getting a good deal?" exists, the only meaningful comparison will be after the Final Plans & Specifications, as outlined in Chapter 9, are completed. The Feasibility Study and Design Review are considered preliminary and trying to compare one professional to another will be like comparing apples to oranges – there are still too many unknowns.

Shopping with another remodeler after the completion of the Final Plans & Specifications is the only way to get a fair and accurate comparison. In doing so, you will need to use the construction plans, outlined specifications and allowance, or product selection schedule the remodeler has compiled.

Building the Project Twice –

Dispelling the Myth "We Didn't Know What Was Behind the Walls"

Quite often I hear the remark "Remodeling is so expensive because you never know what you're getting into; you never know what's behind the walls."

This remark is far from the truth and in most cases is used as an excuse for not taking the time to properly investigate the existing finishes and conditions of the home before starting construction.

In the Conflict-Free Home Remodeling Process we use a term called "Investigative Surgery."

Investigative Surgery is taking the time to research the as-built conditions of the project site in greater detail. For example, if we are remodeling interior space such as a kitchen (on a first floor) and want to remove some of the existing interior walls, we will need to determine whether or not the floor system (assuming the project is a two-story home) above the wall is (load bearing) resting on top of the wall that will be removed.

In this particular case we would cut out a small portion of the ceiling at the location of the wall to be removed in order to look inside and determine whether or not the floor system rests on top of the wall. If the floor system rests on top of the wall to be removed, we can then determine the appropriate engineering solution needed to support the floor system and allow the wall to be removed.

Methods are available to locate unknown underground utilities such as electric lines, water lines, gas lines, etc. prior to the construction of the project. In many instances, an electrician or plumber can crawl under the home or in the attic to investigate the condition of wiring and pipes for their respective areas of work. Investigation of existing materials and conditions allows the remodeler to more accurately prepare for what actually needs to be completed.

Up-Front Remodeling

Proactive investigation by a remodeler can save the homeowner thousands of dollars of unnecessary addendums presented during the course of construction. This method of investigative surgery is part of building the project twice – once on paper and once in the field. The more we build on paper, add on paper, change on paper, and decide on paper, the less we will need to add, change, or decide in the field during construction. The end result to the homeowner is a more accurate estimate of what the costs will be prior to starting construction, and fewer surprises during the course of construction.

Why Remodelers Do Not Spend Time Doing Investigative Surgery

Typically most remodelers do not spend time doing investigative surgery because they do not receive any sort of financial compensation until the project begins, that is, when construction begins. The goal, then, for most remodelers is to get the project into construction as quickly as possible as there is no incentive to spend time up front.

The Conflict-Free Home Remodeling Process that we introduce in Chapter 9 of this book encourages both the remodeler and homeowner to spend more time in the Pre Construction phase, and less time in the Construction phase. This means the homeowner will need to invest a portion of the cost of the project in the Pre Construction phase including hiring the remodeler to do the investigative work required to answer the necessary questions in order to produce a more accurate estimate for the cost of the project.

As the homeowner, you are simply reallocating a small portion of funds that will be used during construction for Pre Construction research.

The fees paid for Pre Construction research will then be credited to the cost of construction when the project goes into Construction. If for any reason during the Pre Construction phase, due to the results of the investigative surgery or other research, you decide the project is too expensive, the project can be abandoned.

Both you and the remodeler win. You win because you have avoided starting construction prematurely. No homeowner wants to find out during construction that the project is too costly to complete. The remodeler wins because he has been paid for his professional time to help reveal those findings to you.

Who's Who – The Architect's Role in Your Remodel

In this chapter, we will discuss the different names used to describe the term "architect." This is the individual responsible for designing the project floor plan and elevations. The "architect" is also the individual who completes the final construction drawings used in the Construction phase of a remodeling process and fulfills the drawing requirements used to obtain a building permit.

Architect

An architect is an individual who designs homes or buildings and, in some cases, participates in overseeing the construction of the home or building designed.

An architect is someone who has completed four years of college education and received a Bachelor of Arts or Bachelor of Science degree in architectural studies. Additionally, it is recognized that an architect who goes on to earn a Master of Architecture degree is qualified to become a licensed architect. Some universities offer a 5-year program called a Bachelor of Architecture, also qualifying for licensure. To acquire licensure, an architect must pass an exam in the particular state in which he or she wishes to be licensed.

 **THE AMERICAN INSTITUTE OF ARCHITECTS**

In many cases, architects who acquire licensure join the *American Institute of Architects (AIA)*. The AIA offers a whole host of resources for the licensed architect to continually learn and stay up to date in the profession of architecture.

Up-Front Remodeling

Residential Designer

The term residential designer means an individual who designs new custom homes, remodels, or additions to existing residential dwellings. Residential designers require no formal education or training in the field of residential design or architecture. Anyone can call himself/herself a residential designer.

For a residential designers to distinguish themselves above their peers and advance to another level, the **American Institute of Building Design (AIBD)**, offers the resources to do so. Most AIBD residential designers strive to educate themselves in a manner which produces the most technically correct and architecturally pleasing custom homes, remodels, and additions.

Draftsman

I want to mention another category of individuals who design homes, additions, and remodels – draftsmen. Draftsmen are sometimes employed by architects and residential designers to complete technical aspects of the construction plans. Some draftsmen are more familiar with technical drawings needed in commercial construction for mechanical, electrical, or plumbing plans conceived by a licensed engineer. Some draftsmen venture out on their own, designing custom homes and additions.

If good architectural balance and features or good space planning is important to you, then I suggest working with an architect or residential designer.

Creativity Versus Technical Knowledge

When selecting an architect or residential designer to create a remodel or addition to your home – whether he or she is an independent or working through your remodeler – it is important to note the two personalities required to complete the documentation necessary to successfully build the project. The two personalities necessary are the creative and the technical – the right and left brain. It is possible but hard to find both personalities in one person.

▶ Creativity

Creativity is the artistic side to architecture. Creativity is the big picture, the right side of the brain. Creativity is taking the existing facade of a 1950s ranch-style home and redesigning it to create a fresh and stunning look. Creativity is taking an awkward floor plan and redesigning the space flow much more harmoniously or incorporating Feng Shui into the mix. Creative architecture is much more fluid, and while the space or elevations are defined, they are not detailed.

The creative architect is the individual who produces the conceptual plan or preliminary plan. This gives the homeowner a first glimpse and general understanding of what the new improvements will look like in the simplest of terms.

▶ Technical

The technical side of architecture is the details – the left side of the brain. This architect takes the big picture and breaks it down into little pieces, making sure one part interacts with the next part. It was once said a good architect is one who can design a building that doesn't leak water.

The technical architect can make sure the building doesn't leak. The technical architect analyzes each and every space in detail to make sure it can actually be built.

The technical architect takes the conceptual or preliminary plan from the creative architect and creates the working set of drawings. All of the work done on the technical side is, in many cases, meaningless to the homeowner but absolutely necessary to the remodeler and the trades and suppliers working to complete the remodel or addition.

Either/Or

If you work with a one-person design team, chances are he or she may be good at both disciplines but probably not excellent at either. My most successful projects have been with architectural firms who have separate creative and technical personalities working at the firm.

You will find many of the most successful home remodels and additions are ones where the remodeler recommends the architect or residential designer to the homeowner or contracts with the architect or residential designer to manage the design process.

It is very important to convey to the remodeler the goals you have in mind for your project. Is the project a simple one-room addition onto the existing house where the architecture is simply matched to the existing architecture? In this case a technical architect may be sufficient and little creative input is required.

If, however, the project is a whole house remodel requiring a new facade on an old tired look, certainly a creative architect is necessary to accomplish this type of remodel. It would then be important for a technical partner in that architect's firm to create the final construction drawings.

Critical Team Member

Whether you hire an outside architect or enter into an agreement with the remodeler to complete the design work, the architect is a critical team member. Discussion should occur regarding the architect's credentials and ability to complete the intended goals.

As the homeowner, if you choose to hire the architect, you will be most successful if you include the remodeler in the selection process. Asking for the remodeler's opinion gives him or her a partnership with whoever is selected and promotes a more team-like atmosphere.

If you allow the remodeler to make the decision about which architect he or she thinks is most suited to provide the design and architecture, you certainly should take the opportunity to meet the individual or team of people who will be working with you to take your ideas and convert them into drawings.

In either case, whether you recommend the architect or your remodeler does, as the homeowner, you should feel comfortable expressing your vision and goals. ***A good architect listens to the homeowners and works hard to create design solutions that ultimately meet their vision and goals.***

Who's Who – The Interior Designer's Role in Your Remodel

Just as between the architect and the residential designer, there is a difference between the interior designer and the interior decorator.

Interior Designer

Typically, by definition, an interior designer is one who has completed a bachelor's degree in interior design and who is qualified to sit for and pass a state exam in order to be called a licensed interior designer. Not all states require interior designers to be licensed, nor do they all offer licensing exams.

Interior designers plan the interior of a space – horizontally and vertically. Interior designers are trained to read blueprints and assess the horizontal space in a proposed floor plan in such a way to ensure that the proposed spaces will accommodate the owner's furniture and accessories. Additionally, interior designers will look at the vertical spaces – the walls of the space – to determine the placement of architectural details such as mouldings, built-in bookcases, locations of windows and doors in relationship to the floor space, and the location of artwork and accessories. Interior designers are also responsible for specifying all of the products (i.e. plumbing fixtures, electrical fixtures, tile, cabinets, countertops, etc.) and colors of the products to be installed in the project.

Another important function of an interior designer is the designer's capability for drawing by hand or on CAD (computer-aided design) the details necessary for the remodeler to install the specified products. For example, tile for a bathroom may be specified to be installed in a shower and may include trim pieces and inlays. The interior designer will draw the location for installation of each of the tiles and trim pieces. The interior designer will also specify the location and positioning of wood mouldings. Bookcases and built-ins are also designed and detailed by interior designers. How you interact and live within your home is the

Up-Front Remodeling

interior designer's specialty – he or she will give drawings showing how moving a window three feet will achieve the goal of having a reading nook in the bedroom.

American Society of Interior Designers

The most qualified interior designers are typically ones who join the association called **American Society of Interior Design (ASID)**. To become a professional ASID member, one needs to have completed a course of accredited education and equivalent work experience in interior design and have passed the National Council for Interior Design Qualification (NCIDQ) examination. Upon successful completion of the examination, one can be called a professional member of the American Society of Interior Design.

Membership in ASID offers the interior designer a whole host of educational opportunities and support to keep the designer at the forefront of the interior design profession.

Interior Decorator

An interior decorator is not required to have completed any formal education in order to call himself / herself an interior decorator. Interior decorators are most helpful in specifying and selecting the products needed in an addition or remodel (i.e., plumbing fixtures, electrical fixtures, tile, cabinets, countertops, etc.) and colors of the products to be installed in the project.

While some interior decorators will offer the services similar to that of an interior designer, there is no guarantee they have been formally trained in those particular areas.

Another professional, sometimes used in the design process, is an interior designer who focuses specifically on the kitchen and bath areas of the home. Professionally, this person is called a CKD (Certified Kitchen Designer), CBD (Certified Bathroom Designer), or, if certified in both areas, a CMKBD (Certified Master Kitchen and Bath Designer).

These certifications are administered by **The National Kitchen & Bath Association (NKBA)**, an association for kitchen and bath professionals. These certified designers are either independent designers or work for a local kitchen and bathroom cabinet company. NKBA certification is based on in-depth testing and extensive industry experience. NKBA certified designers must also meet annual continuing education requirements.

The NKBA certifies kitchen and bath design professionals in various stages of expertise:

AKBD® – An Associate Kitchen and Bath Designer is a certified professional with a minimum of 2 years of kitchen/bath industry experience – he or she is knowledgeable in product selection, space planning, materials, and finishes. An AKBD must meet specific educational requirements, as well as pass a comprehensive academic exam.

CKD® – Certified Kitchen Designers have a minimum of 7 years experience designing residential kitchen spaces. They are highly skilled in design, space planning, and product selection, and have extensive knowledge of building codes, flooring materials, appliances, and mechanical systems. They write specifications and draw plans that are easily interpreted by plumbers, electricians, and installers. A CKD must meet specific educational requirements and pass a comprehensive academic and practical exam.

CBD® - Certified Bathroom Designers also have a minimum of 7 years experience designing residential bathroom spaces – they are highly skilled in design, space planning, and product selection, and have extensive knowledge of building codes, fixtures, flooring materials, and mechanical/plumbing systems. They write specifications and draw plans that are easily interpreted by plumbers, electricians, and installers. A CBD must meet specific educational requirements, as well as pass a comprehensive academic and practical exam.

CMKBD® – A Certified Master Kitchen and Bath Designer is a designer who has obtained both CKD and CBD certification, has over 10 years of kitchen /bath industry experience, and has been nationally recognized through design competitions, industry awards, printed publications, or television spots. A CMKBD must also meet specific educational requirements.

National Kitchen & Bath Association certification definitions taken from the NKBA website: www.nkba.org

A kitchen and bath designer can design independently if the project is a stand-alone kitchen or bathroom remodel, or, work with an interior designer or decorator as part of a design team.

Critical Team Member

Some homeowners prefer to act as their own interior designer or decorator. Although the interior designer is viewed as an optional player in planning for a successful remodel, he or she is one one of the most overlooked and underappreciated players in the process. While we have had successful projects where the homeowner has acted as the interior designer, our most dramatic projects have included a professional interior designer. An interior designer often finds ways to make a room more functional and pleasing to the eye.

Up-Front Remodeling

One interior designer with whom I work is excellent with color; any time I have a homeowner in need of a repaint I refer him. This particular interior designer is so good I have had people stop by my home to ask me for the color palette for the exterior of my home (it includes four colors) because they liked it so much. Additionally, I have had people contact me from around the country asking for colors they have seen in projects on my website.

Paint is paint, tile is tile, and a sink faucet is a sink faucet. Homeowners can use the same priced paint, tile and plumbing fixtures and decide for themselves what brand, profile, or color to use. The remodeler will purchase these products and install them according to the wishes of the homeowners.

However, use a creative interior designer and the difference can be dramatically different; the products and colors can pop and come alive like nothing you could have imagined. The difference is like night and day.

The interior designer plays an important role in the Design Review step of the Pre Construction phase.

Why Choosing the Remodeler First Makes Sense

The Remodeler Is the Conductor

In the previous chapters, we discussed the difference between the architect and residential designer and the difference between the interior designer and interior decorator. An architect (whether provided in-house by the remodeler or outsourced) is certain for any project's design. The question is: When do you bring in the architect and interior designer?

In residential remodeling, the remodeler that plans the project on paper with the homeowner is the leader of the planning phase of the project. This clearly becomes evident as we consider all the people the remodeler will work with in this chapter to plan your remodel. When we review The Conflict-Free Home Remodeling Process in Chapter 9 of this book, you'll learn that choosing the remodeler first is the most logical way to collect all the necessary information to know all the details and costs before construction. The remodeler should certainly be the first person contacted when embarking on any remodeling project since this is the one professional who regularly interacts with all the other professionals, departments and groups to plan a project. Throughout the planning process of a remodeling project, or as we call it the Pre Construction phase, the remodeler, based on the complexity of the project, will have contact and interaction with some or all of the following professionals:

- ▶ Architect
- ▶ Interior Designer
- ▶ Health Department
- ▶ Structural Engineer
- ▶ Trades
- ▶ Building Materials Suppliers
- ▶ Finish Materials Suppliers
- ▶ Surveyor
- ▶ Zoning Department
- ▶ Landscape Designer
- ▶ Water Management Districts
- ▶ Arborist
- ▶ Homeowners Association
- ▶ Historic Preservation Board
- ▶ Building Department

Up-Front Remodeling

Let's take a look at each one of the professionals:

Architect
On a smaller more defined remodeling project or addition, the architect may be behind the scenes and never need to interact with the homeowner. The remodeler will simply interpret the outlined plan and scope of work to the architect. In a larger, more involved, whole-house remodel, where a higher level of creativity is needed, the architect in most cases will have face-to-face interaction with the homeowner along with the input of the remodeler.

Interior Designer
If the homeowner decides it is necessary to retain an interior designer to assist in the selections of products and finishes, the remodeler will work very closely with the interior designer to make sure all necessary products or finishes requiring owner approval are outlined and addressed in order for the homeowner to make the appropriate selections prior to starting construction.

Landscape Designer
If the remodel or addition impacts or includes any of the existing three parts of landscape (vegetation, irrigation, or hardscape), a landscape designer can be considered.

1. Vegetation – including grass and plants that will be planted on or around the structural improvements to the property.
2. Irrigation – the underground or above-ground watering system used to keep the plants and vegetation alive.
3. Hardscape – driveways, walkways, retaining walls, planters, and fountains.

Structural Engineer
In most states and municipalities where a building permit is required, the plans submitted to the building department typically require the seal of a registered or certified engineer in that particular state. Engineering on a residential addition or remodel, in addition to other items, includes the size and makeup of the foundation on which the building will be constructed and the framing materials, type and size, and fasteners needed to assemble the walls, floor and roof structure. There are many ways to achieve the final look of the desired project while using particular materials and building methods that may reduce the actual cost to the homeowner. These practices and methods are discussed between the remodeler and structural engineer.

Trades
The trades are a collection of craftsmen and their companies who will perform all the necessary tasks required to complete the desired scope of work. Based on the simplicity or complexity of any given project, the remodeler will choose the particular team player, or trade, to complete that particular task in the most economical fashion possible. In many cases, the trades will consult with the remodeler during the Pre Construction phase to determine the most appropriate method of construction for a particular area.

Chapter 6. Why Choosing the Remodeler First Makes Sense

Building Materials Suppliers

Building materials suppliers are the companies who supply the building materials necessary to complete the work – many materials located behind the walls within the structure, which will never be seen by the homeowner. Similar to the trades, based on the simplicity or complexity of any given project, the remodeler will recommend the necessary building supplies from the appropriate company. Also, similar to the trades, building suppliers will in many cases consult with the remodeler during the Pre Construction phase in order to specify the appropriate material for any given area of the project.

Finish Materials Suppliers

Finish materials suppliers are the companies who provide the materials or products located in the areas of the home that the homeowner and their guests will see. Some of these products include cabinets, plumbing fixtures, floor coverings, and electrical fixtures. It is very important, based on the homeowner's budget, for the remodeler to refer or recommend the homeowner to the appropriate suppliers who can meet both the visual and budgetary requirements of the homeowner.

Surveyor

The remodeler will work directly with the surveyor in order to determine the practicality for additions onto an existing house as it relates to topography, setbacks, floor to area ratio, and impervious coverage. Sometimes this research is coordinated by the architect.

Zoning Department

If, based on information obtained through the surveyor, the remodeler determines the scope of work is outside of the established guidelines for that municipality, the remodeler will work with the municipal zoning department on the homeowner's behalf to submit requests for variances. Sometimes this process is coordinated by the architect.

Health Department

Many homeowners are surprised to learn the health department may be involved in their home remodel or addition project. If the project includes relocating or upgrading a septic system, the remodeler will get the necessary documentation required to submit for the appropriate permits to modify or add onto an existing septic system.

Water Management Districts

If an addition to an existing home includes exterior construction in or close to a wetland area or adjacent to a lakefront, stream, or other body of water, certain water management districts may need to be consulted by the remodeler in order to comply with those particular regulations.

Arborist

If trees are to be removed from the property to make way for improvements to the property, an arbor permit may be required. It may be necessary to document what tree(s) will be removed and what you will be planting in place of trees removed by the remodeler.

Up-Front Remodeling

Homeowners Association

The remodeler will work with the neighborhood or condominium association to make sure the approval process is followed for any exterior addition or improvement subject to architectural review board, design review committee, or similar entity. In some cases, the requirements determined by a neighborhood architectural review board are more stringent than the local zoning or building department. In some situations, homeowners' associations may be dealt with by the architect.

Historic Preservation Board

In neighborhoods where the home is deemed historic, there are additional sets of rules, regulations and guidelines the homeowner and remodeler must follow in order to comply with a historic preservation district. These guidelines almost always apply to exterior remodels, additions, or other improvements to the existing exterior of a home, The remodeler will need to access and review these guidelines in order to plan more appropriately for the homeowner's desired scope of work. Similar to homeowners' associations, historic preservation boards may be dealt with by the architect.

Building Department

Finally, when all of the above has been discussed, debated, deliberated, applied for, and approved, the remodeler will complete the building permit application and all of the above will be submitted to the building department for its review. The remodeler will continue to submit revisions, clarifications and any other supplemental information required by the building department in order for the remodeler on behalf of the homeowner, to receive the building department's final blessing so that a building permit is issued and construction can commence.

Because of the amount of time and competence required, you now know why there are unlicensed remodelers and homeowners who prefer to bypass the entire permitting process and construct an addition or remodel to their home without the involvement of governmental agencies. *That said, all of the above participants in the building permit process and Pre Construction phase are designed and in place to make sure the outcome of your project is successful and safe for you.*

When you go through a predetermined Pre Construction phase with a professional remodeler, the benefits to you include:
- ▶ *An addition or remodel much more integrated into the existing home.*
- ▶ *Much better resale value for future consideration.*
- ▶ *The ability to resell the home because you will be assured the new structure or improvements will have met the required municipal guidelines allowing you to sell the home without an encumbrance of title restricting you from the sale of the home to another person.*

If a remodeler bypasses certain government stipulated requirements and deficiencies are found during a home inspection, corrective work may be required prior to the sale of the home.

The remodeler is the conductor of the orchestra and the musicians are the departments and people listed above. It is up to the remodeler to choose the most appropriate instrument or player in every area so the outcome is beautiful music – a beautiful, well-balanced, well-thought-out and constructed remodel or addition.

Chapter 6. Why Choosing the Remodeler First Makes Sense

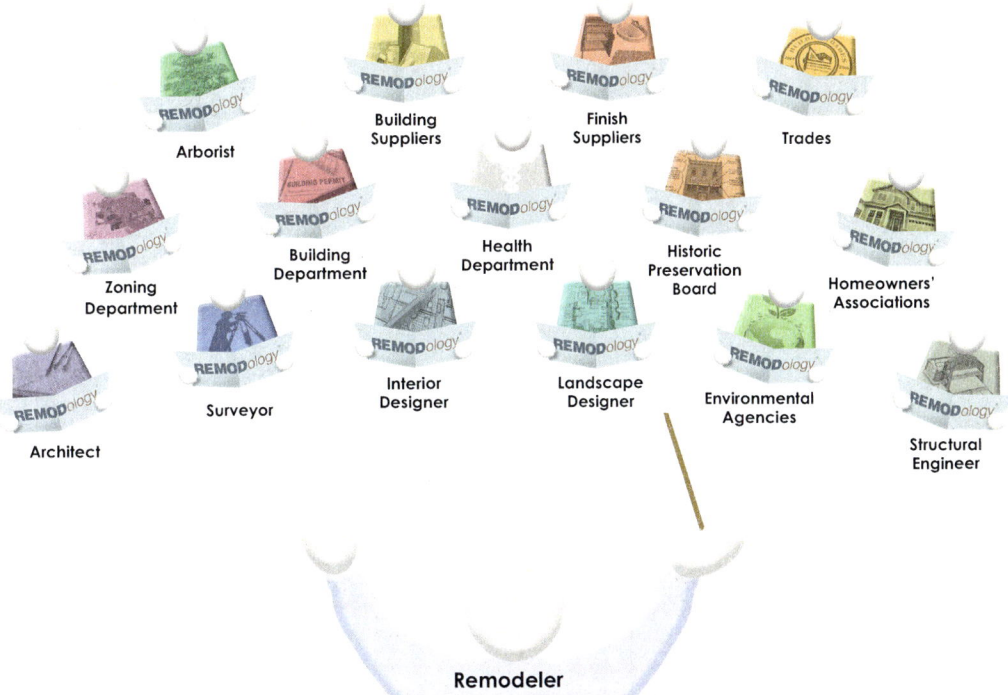

In residential remodeling, by default, the remodeler is the person addressing and communicating with all of the above departments, agencies and associated companies. The remodeler must be knowledgeable about everything going on around the project and understand how each one is related to the project in order to make the appropriate decisions to accomplish the homeowner's desired goals. *In residential remodeling, the remodeler is indeed the conductor; the entire process and all other departments, agencies and associated companies are the musicians – together making beautiful music.* Certainly, before embarking on this necessary but time-consuming process, there must be a way to determine whether or not the project is even feasible. Investing a small amount of time, energy and money can determine that. *The Conflict-Free Home Remodeling Process begins by finding the right remodeler and then uses the step-by-step Home Remodeling Process to determine if your desired scope of work is realistic based on your set of criteria.*

Choosing the Right Remodelor – Is the Chemistry Right?

Finding the Right Remodelor

The Conflict-Free Home Remodeling Process is designed so you and your remodeler begin on common ground with the same expectations and outcome in mind.

It is still very important to take the time to investigate and search for the right remodeling company for your project. You want to make sure your personalities connect and the chemistry is right. You will be spending a lot of time with this company and the people who work for the company.

Some topics of discussion or questions to ask prior to selecting the right remodeler include:

- ▶ Number of years in business
- ▶ Proof of license (if required by the state or municipality)
- ▶ Proof of insurances – general liability and workers' compensation (if required by the state or municipality)
- ▶ Established presence in the community
- ▶ Permanent mailing address
- ▶ Solid relationships with trades and suppliers
- ▶ Prompt resolution of prior problems
- ▶ Working knowledge of type of project
- ▶ Portfolio photos
- ▶ Referrals for type of project
- ▶ Type of warranty

Additional Clues to Finding the Right Remodelor

▶ Website

Look at the prospective company's website. This will tell you a lot about the remodeler's style, professionalism, and work history. The website is also a good place to find out additional information about the history of the company and its philosophy related to the remodeling industry.

Up-Front Remodeling

▶ **Home Builders Association**

Membership and involvement in a local home builders association, such as one affiliated with The ***National Association of Home Builders***, indicates the remodeler is not isolated and is open to networking with other individuals in the home building and remodeling industry. Home Builders Associations offer educational opportunities to help the remodeler stay abreast of the most current building code regulations, construction technologies, green building practices, and many other forms of information which can be used towards creating a better project for the homeowner. *From NAHB website*

▶ **Remodelers**

Membership with NAHB Remodelers reflects a remodeler's commitment to responsible business practices, quality construction, and reliable customer service. With industry-leading programs in education, networking, marketing advocacy, and recognition or excellence, NAHB Remodelers gives you the tools you need to build your remodeling business. *From NAHB website*

▶ **National Association of The Remodeling Industry**

NARI's core purpose is to advance and promote the remodeling industry's professionalism, product & vital public purpose. NARI's focus is on professional conduct, continuing education and training, and fair and ethical treatment within the industry. *From NARI website*

▶ **Certifications and Designations**

Certifications indicate your remodeler has the desire to learn as much as possible about the remodeling industry and the resources available. This, in turn, means he or she is better equipped to assist you in making more informed decisions, resulting in a more efficient project, at a better value to you.

▶ **Neighborhood Projects**

A drive-by of projects the remodeler has in progress will give you a good indication of what your project will look like during construction. A tidy-looking job site with the construction areas well delineated shows that the remodeler cares about the homeowner he or she is working for, as well as the surrounding neighbors.

▶ **Referrals**

Asking around the community will reveal the most prominent remodeling companies in your community. Checking with realtors, new home builders, and suppliers of construction materials, and asking them who they would choose to remodel their homes is a great indicator of whom you should choose.

▶ Remodeling Versus New Home Construction

What percentage of the remodeler's work is focused on remodeling versus new home construction? It is important the remodeler has a strong track record with remodeling work.

Choose Carefully

The reality of remodeling, or adding on to your home is, you are "marrying" your remodeler - not for life, although sometimes it feels that way - for three months, six months, twelve months, or as long as it takes to complete your remodeling goals. Your remodeler will come to know you and everyone in your family on a very close level.

For this reason, it is so important the "courting phase," or in this case the Pre Construction phase of the project, be a very meaningful and in-depth part of the construction process.

For many reasons, some illustrated in this book, the typical remodeler all too often rushes to the "altar" and begins construction without listening to or understanding the homeowner's true needs and concerns. Inevitably this lack of communication - not asking questions and truly discovering the wants, needs, desires, concerns, goals, or real budget of the homeowner - leads to tense relationships and so often a broken relationship between the homeowner and the remodeler.

The Conflict-Free Home Remodeling Process is inherently designed to ask the questions and discover the wants, needs, desires, concerns, and goals in the Pre Construction phase and allow the homeowner's expectations to be revealed and understood by the remodeler so that the remodeler may appropriately plan for a successful remodeling project.

Comparing the Cost for a Remodel/Addition to the Cost for New Home Construction

NOTE: Costs noted in this chapter are for illustrative purposes only and are not accurately reflected in all geographic areas.

In over 20 years of preparing for and presenting budgets to homeowners, I find a majority of homeowners are completely overwhelmed at what I think it will cost (more) for their project versus what they think it should cost (less).

Regardless of whom I speak with, everyone has an opinion of how much their project should cost. I find that opinion is mostly based on the square foot cost of their home when it was built new – sometimes 10 to 20 years ago - or the square foot cost of other homes in today's market. *Using the square foot method for pricing an addition or remodel is a risky and inaccurate way of evaluating the true cost of an addition or remodel.*

Square Foot Cost Defined

Square foot cost is defined by the cost of the home divided by the square feet of floor space in the home. Even this is ambiguous because it can be calculated at least four different ways. Let's look at those four ways.

We will use an example of a 2,500 square foot home valued at $250,000. Let's assume the land, or the building lot, for the home costs $25,000. This means the home costs $300,000 to construct.

When we examine square feet, in this case 2,500 square feet, we are speaking of only the living space in the house; living space as opposed to total space under roof. The living space in a home is usually defined by the amount of area heated and/or cooled by a heating or air conditioning system. Living space does not include covered entries to the home, garages and porches, or balconies. These spaces are sometimes referred to as non-living or un-air conditioned spaces under roof.

Let's assume for this 2,500 square feet of living space, there will be an additional 1,000 square feet of space under roof, bringing the total amount of space under roof to 3,500 square feet.

Up-Front Remodeling

Let's recap this information:

Values

Value of home $250,000
Value of land $25,000
Total value of home and land $275,000

Square Feet Calculations

Square feet of heated and cooled living space 2,500
Square feet of non-heated and cooled space 1,000
Square feet of total space under roof 3,500

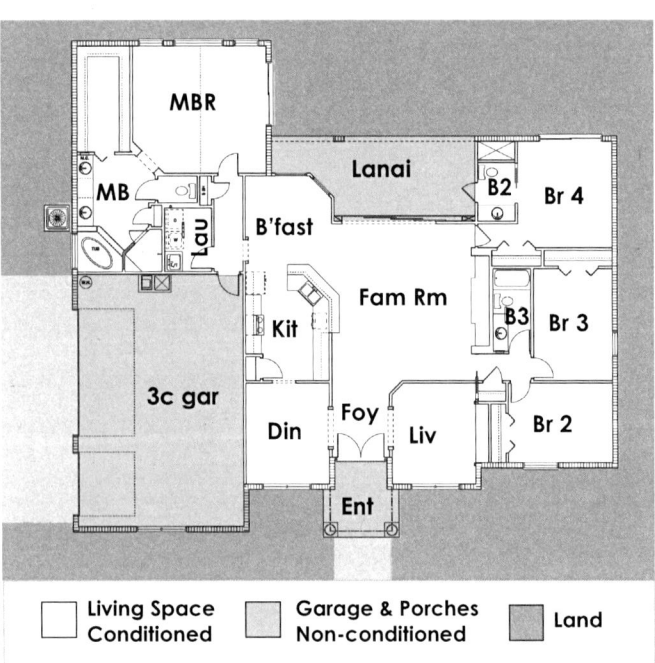

Given this information, here are four methods in which cost per square foot can be calculated:

1. Total cost of home and land, divided by square feet of heated and cooled living space:
$275,000 / 2,500 sf = $110 per square foot.

2. Total cost of home not including land, divided by square feet of heated and cooled living space:
$250,000 / 2,500 sf = $100 per square foot.

3. Total cost of the home and land, divided by square feet of space under roof:
$275,000 / 3,500 sf = $78.57 per square foot.

4. Total cost of home not including land, divided by square feet of space under roof:
$250,000 / 3,500 sf = $71.43 per square foot.

The most accurate of the four methods are methods #2 and #4, because they are both reflective of the construction costs for the building only and do not include the cost of the land.

It is very important not to get too caught up with the square foot cost of a remodel or addition. There are quite a few variables specific to remodels and additions that should be considered. These variables have a way of distorting the comparison of new construction to remodels and additions.

Additional Factors Impacting Remodels and Additions

Using a square-foot dollar amount to begin with might sound reasonable when creating a budget; however, let's look at six particular areas that add to the cost of a remodel or addition and why it costs more – per square foot – than building a new home.

1. Access to the Project
2. Protecting Existing Finishes
3. Economy of Scale
4. Tie-in to Existing Space
5. Remodel of Existing Space
6. Supervision

1. Access to the Project

In a large number of cases, the remodeling project is located at the back of the home. In new construction, in most cases, material delivery trucks can back onto the project site and simply offload the materials close to the desired location where those materials will be used.

Often in new construction, concrete trucks, for example, can back up to the desired area and pour the concrete right from the truck into the finished area. The company delivering the block can maneuver the forklift onto the new concrete floor and strategically place the pallet of block next to the areas where they will be used. The drywall delivery truck can back up close to the home and position the boom loaded with drywall next to the window to be easily offloaded.

With a remodeling project, the concrete truck typically cannot drive on to the property and the concrete needs to be carried by hand via a wheelbarrow. Or a pump truck needs to be brought in to pump the concrete from the concrete truck located at the curb to the area of construction. Because the block forklift is usually too wide to maneuver alongside an existing home, the block needs to be carried by hand from the delivery truck at the curb to the construction area. The same is true for the drywall delivery. Each and every board will need to be carried by hand to the construction area.

These are only three of many other possible examples in which additional labor is required to move materials from the delivery area to the construction site. This additional labor required adds to the cost of a remodel or addition.

Access to an addition constructed at the back of a home

2. Protecting Existing Finishes

In new construction, there is no existing home to protect. ***With a remodel or addition, a remodeler should always consider "How will I protect the homeowner and family from the construction work if they are living there day and night?"*** This is one of the remodeler's biggest challenges, and, of course, it also creates additional costs to the project. Included here are a few areas of concern that remodelers examine when embarking on an addition or remodel to an existing home.

Up-Front Remodeling

Interior Living Space

In many cases, temporary walls will need to be erected inside the home to separate the living area from the construction area. Many remodelers use 2x4 wood and plywood materials to build temporary walls with doors and locks to protect the homeowner and family from the construction work and debris.

Interior of homeowners' living space protected by a temporary plywood wall and door

Landscaping & Irrigation

Temporary fencing is installed to create a logical and efficient pathway allowing workers to access the construction area while creating minimum compromise to the landscaping and irrigation system on the property.

Pool

Exposed pool decks are covered with plywood to protect the finished surface. Temporary half walls made of 2x4 wood and plywood are built around the pool on top of the temporary plywood deck to protect the pool from debris.

3. Economies of Scale

In any type of manufacturing, larger quantity orders are proportionally less expensive than single or lower quantity orders.

Let's use concrete as an example: a poured-in-place, on the ground, concrete slab. The workers have prepared the ground, installed the form boards in which the concrete is to be poured, chemically treated the soil, placed the plastic vapor barrier over the soil, and laid the wire reinforcing mesh. The surface is prepared and the concrete is ready to be poured.

In the example of a 3500-square-foot new home (under roof), it would take six men approximately ten hours (60 man hours) to set up, pour the concrete from the concrete delivery truck, finish the concrete, and clean up. Using a fictitious rate of $35 per-man-hour times 60 hours, the cost of labor for this particular task would be $2,100 or a labor rate of $0.60 ($2,100 / 3500 sf = $0.60) per square foot of surface area.

In comparison, if we have a 500-square-foot addition located in the back of an existing home, it would take two men approximately eight hours (16 man hours) to set up, move by hand or pump the concrete from street (from the concrete delivery truck), finish the concrete, and clean up. Using the same fictitious rate of $35 per-man-hour times 16 hours, the cost of labor for this particular task would be $560 or a labor rate of $1.12 ($560 / 500 = $1.12) per square foot of surface area.

Additionally, the remodeler would pay two premiums; one to the concrete company, approximately $75-$100, for sending out a less than full truck (short load) of concrete. The second premium would be to the concrete pump company to set up and pump from the street – much more efficient than using a wheelbarrow and moving the concrete by hand from the street at the front of the home. This premium would cost approximately $200. The two premiums (not necessary for most new homes) total $275 divided by the square foot size of the addition of 500 equal an additional $0.55 ($275/500= $0.55) per square foot.

Concrete Installation – New Home vs. Addition

(Installation of concrete only; does not include preparation of the surface to be poured)

New Home 3500 sf	Addition 500 sf
Labor cost............$2,100	Labor cost.............$560
	Short load $75
	Concrete pump...$200
Total cost..............$2,100	Total cost...............$835
Divided By	Divided By
Square foot size.....3,500	Square foot size......500
Cost per sf..............$0.60	Cost per sf............$1.67

The total square-foot cost for the concrete labor, short load, and pump for the addition is $1.67 per square foot. In this one example alone, the remodeler's costs are almost 3 times or 300% more than a new home.

Other examples of areas impacted by the economies of scale and increased labor pricing include:
▶ Framing labor
▶ Siding or exterior stucco labor
▶ Roofing labor
▶ Insulation installation
▶ Drywall or plaster installation
▶ Trim carpentry labor
▶ Painting

Normally, the economies of scale are affected primarily by labor. Typically, material costs are not affected as drastically as labor. As in the example of the concrete, the additional charges for materials are in the delivery fees for smaller quantities of product. Additionally, moving materials from the delivery truck to the staging site can increase material costs.

4. Tie-in to Existing Space

I cannot think of an addition I have completed where there is not a tie-in to the existing space. ***Even additions that are not physically attached to the existing home or structure usually have mechanical tie-ins such as plumbing and electric.*** Let's look at a few of many areas we take into consideration when adding onto an existing home.

Roof Trusses and Roofing Material

In cases where the roof lines on the addition are at the same height as the roof lines on the existing home, the structural roof system will be tied into the existing structural roofing system. This structural link creates the need for additional wood framing materials as well as labor to tie the new structural roof system into the existing roof.

Up-Front Remodeling

Additional quantities of roof shingles or roof tiles and labor to install those materials will be incurred, and the new roof will need to be woven into the existing roof.

Plumbing Supply and Waste Lines

If the addition or remodel requires plumbing for a kitchen, bathroom, or wet bar, the need for hot and cold running water and waste lines will be necessary. The existing hot and cold water supply lines will need to be located and tapped and new lines connected to the new plumbing locations.

In many cases, it may not be possible to tie the new waste line into the existing waste line at the closest location. The closest waste line may also not be the correct size (too small) to match the size of the new waste line. In some cases, a trench may need to be dug outside along the existing home to the front of the property so the new waste line can be tied into the existing main waste line.

Electrical Service

Electrical wires from the new addition will either need to be run (installed) and connected to an existing breaker panel, or an additional main electrical supply cable will need to be run to a new breaker panel located in the new addition.

Connecting to the Existing Home

In many cases, the point of connection from the existing home into the new addition will be made:
▶ Through an existing window modified into a door.
▶ Through an existing exterior door. The door is removed and the opening modified to look like an interior door rather than an exterior door.
▶ Cutting an opening through the existing exterior wall adjoining the new addition, to create a new passage way.

When connecting an addition to an existing home, these are just a few examples that may be applicable and will impact the project cost.

5. Remodeling or Modification of Existing Space

We just finished speaking about tying into existing space and the impact that has on the project budget. In many cases, we find the room adjacent to the addition may also require modifications. Sometimes it may be as simple as new paint and carpet. In other cases, it will require new walls, doors, trim, or other finished materials.

Depending on the extent of the necessary work, remodeling, or modification to existing spaces can create a very large difference in the proposed budget for the new addition.

6. Supervision

In this chapter, when we speak about protection of existing finishes, tie-in to existing, or remodel of existing space, we are also speaking of a considerable amount of additional supervision and management to get those things done effectively and successfully.

The remodeler should spend additional time to make sure the existing home is protected from the construction zone. Additional time is required with each trade or craftsman working on the job to discuss the most appropriate and appealing way to tie one part of the house to the other and make it look seamless.

The amount of detail and supervision required in overseeing the successful completion of a remodel or addition is proportionally much more than constructing a new home. Let's look at two examples:

Custom Home Superintendent

Let's assume a custom home builder building 3500-square-foot (under roof) custom homes can expect a superintendent to manage approximately six homes at any given time. Let's also assume the following:

1. Each of the six homes costs $250,000 for the home only (no land cost).
2. It costs the builder $60,000 annually for salary and benefits (and labor burden) for a superintendent.
3. The superintendent can complete the six new homes in nine months.

▶ $60,000 annual salary / 12 months = $5,000 per month

▶ $5,000 per month x 9 months = approximately $45,000 / 6 homes = $7,500 per home

It costs the new home builder $45,000 in supervision to manage these six homes, or $7,500 per home.

Remodeling Superintendent

Comparatively, a remodeling superintendent, because of the added level of difficulty and necessary oversight required, can effectively manage approximately 4 projects at any given time, based on the following assumptions:

1. Each remodeling project has an average value of $100,000.
2. It costs the remodeler the same annual salary and benefits (and labor burden) of $60,000 for a superintendent.
3. The superintendent can complete the four projects in five months.

▶ $60,000 annual salary / 12 months = $5,000 per month

▶ $5,000 x 5 months = $25,000 / 4 projects = $6,250 per project

It costs the remodeler $25,000 in supervision to manage these four projects, or $6,250 per project.

Up-Front Remodeling

Comparative Results

Now, at first glance it appears to cost less for supervision of the remodel versus the new home - $6,250 per remodel versus $7,500 per new home. However when you look at the cost based on the value of the project, we get a different story.

	Supervision Per Home	Cost of New Home or Remodel	Percentage of Cost
New Home	$7,500	/ $250,000	= 3.00%
Remodel	$6,250	/ $100,000	= 6.25%

In this example, it has cost the remodeler (percent of project cost) more than double in supervision costs to manage each remodeling project compared to the new custom home projects. It is fair to say this is an average impact for most remodeling projects.

Costs to Stay or Relocate

The square foot cost example and six additional factors, Access to the Project, Protecting Existing Finishes, Economies of Scale, Tie-in to Existing Space, Remodel of Existing Space, and Supervision, illustrate why it is more expensive, per square foot, to remodel or add on to a home, compared to constructing a new home.

Alternatively, there are costs associated with selling an existing home to move into a new home. They include:
▶ Minor repairs and updates to make the home more desirable for a buyer
▶ Real estate commissions
▶ Loan costs for a new mortgage
▶ Moving expenses

When you look at the net difference, in many cases it may be more cost effective (financially) to add on or to remodel your home than to relocate to another home or purchase a new home. And when you do find the next home, it may not be exactly what you are looking for. *With a remodel you can get exactly what you want. The Conflict-Free Home Remodeling Process that is outlined in Chapter 9 will help you understand what steps must be taken to know if moving or remodeling is in your best interest and which is the most cost effective for you.*

An Overview of the Conflict-Free Home Remodeling Process

The Process at a Glance

In Chapters 1-8 of this book, you have learned how to avoid spending more than you can afford, you now understand why remodeling seems more expensive than new construction, you discovered why putting a project "out to bid" can be a set-up for failure, and finally you now know all of the professionals involved in a remodeling project, plus understand the hierarchy of who's who for your project. In this chapter, we introduce you to the Conflict-Free Home Remodeling Process - the answer to avoiding the home remodeling letdown by knowing all details and costs *before* construction.

Whether you are planning a whole-house remodel with additions, a single addition, or interior remodel or modification, Conflict-Free Home Remodeling, a two-phase, six-step process, logically describes how to plan for and complete a home remodeling project plus how to avoid experiencing letdown along the way. This process ends the "high-drama" we have witnessed on reality home remodeling shows.

The greatest change for the remodeling industry in The Conflict-Free Home Remodeling Process is Phase One, Pre Construction. Historically, the majority of time spent on a project has been in Phase Two, Construction. The Conflict-Free Process takes a closer look and spends more time in the Pre Construction phase of the process in order to ensure a more successful Construction phase and project completion. As we discussed throughout this book, up-front planning is now necessary with increased government regulations and the vast array of choices homeowners have for products and concepts such as Green Building and/or Aging in Place Designs.

The Home Remodeling Process results in spending less money than would otherwise have been spent through unwise and unnecessary decisions during the construction phase of remodeling.

Up-Front Remodeling

The Conflict-Free Home Remodeling Process

Phase One	Pre Construction
Step 1	Feasibility Study
Step 2	Design Review
Step 3	Final Plans & Specifications
Phase Two	**Construction**
Step 1	Construction Preparation
Step 2	Construction
Step 3	Post Construction

REMODology®

Conflict-Free Home Remodeling Outline

Phase One – Pre Construction

Step 1 – Feasibility Study
1. The Initial Call
2. The First Meeting
3. The Presentation

The Feasibility Study is the first of three steps in the Pre Construction portion of The Conflict-Free Home Remodeling Process. The main goal for the Feasibility Study step of The Home Remodeling Process is to determine whether or not the project is feasible for you and your budget. This study is done before hiring the architect. The remodeler's goal is to understand the general idea of what you would like to accomplish and make sure the budget is within range. Then you can focus on the details in the second step of the process.

Step 2 – Design Review
1. Hiring the Architect
2. As-Built Drawings
3. Hardlined Floor Plan
4. Investigative Surgery
5. Reaffirm Budgets

Step two of Pre Construction is Design Review. The architect and interior designer are brought into the process during this step. The purpose of this step is to begin to refine your vision and the scope of work for your home. At the end of this step, you will have a refined preliminary plan, elevations and a more defined budget. During this step of The Home Remodeling Process, it is appropriate for you to add to or subtract from the scope of work. The goal at the end of this step, however, is for you, the homeowner, to have a final decision about the scope of work.

Step 3 – Final Plans & Specifications
1. Final Plans
2. Product Selection
3. Bid Conference
4. Specifications
5. General Conditions
6. Payment Schedule

Step Three of Pre Construction is the beginning of the home stretch of Phase One. Key information in this step will become the final documents from which the remodeler and his or her team of trades and suppliers will work. This step of The Home Remodeling Process is about researching, compiling, refining and presenting all the information necessary to accomplish your dream and goals.

Phase Two – Construction

Step 1 – Construction Preparation
1. Construction Work Schedule
2. Pre Construction Expectations Meeting

Now that a final agreement between the remodeler and yourself has been reached, the actual construction work is ready to begin. Prior to the actual start of construction, a few more items will be addressed between you and the remodeler or completed prior to starting project set-up and demolition.

Step 2 – Construction
Keeping Peace

At this point, the building permits are in hand, the notice of commencement approved and filed, the construction schedule reviewed, and final expectations outlined. The remodeler is now ready to begin the transformation of your home into the agreed scope of work. During construction, there are a few things that will take place to provide you with peace of mind and prepare for the successful completion of the project.

Step 3 – Post Construction
1. The Last Impression
2. Move In and Enjoy

The construction has come to an end. Everything you have planned in the Pre Construction steps of The Conflict-Free Home Remodeling Process has been delivered and is now reality. Before parting ways with the remodeler, there are several items of information you will be given to keep at your home for reference.

Win-Win - Everyone Benefits

Home remodeling is a very complex and invasive business but it can be simplified and done successfully. Strangers whom you have never met will come into your home and walk through your personal spaces, looking inside storage areas, closets, bedrooms, and bathrooms in an effort to help create a more functional and meaningful lifestyle for you in your home.

Your home will literally be turned into a factory where all of the pre-manufactured parts and pieces will be assembled right in front of you. Remodeling a home in our present society with so many choices and so many options to choose from becomes mind-boggling and sometimes overwhelming.

To be successful in today's remodeling world, it takes a well-thought-out and organized process to create the most positive and meaningful results for the homeowner and everyone involved. Remodelers who follow a process that utilizes the appropriate resources, and implements the necessary steps pertaining to each particular project, complete the most successful remodeling projects.

In life, I believe success is partly measured by how many people win in a given situation. In business especially, I know it is very important for all involved parties to feel they have positively benefited from a relationship or project in which they have been involved. Success in a remodeling project is achieved when all parties involved know they have made a positive difference and have personally benefitted from the experience.

Up-Front Remodeling

Architect and Interior Designer

The architect's and interior designer's job is to design the new space for the homeowner. The architect and interior designer are not constantly purchasing building materials or hiring trades*, and may not know current realistic costs for construction.

Using The Conflict-Free Home Remodeling Process, the remodeler becomes the architect's and interior designer's partner. The remodeler is there to work with them to make sure their design becomes a reality, all within the homeowner's goals, vision, and budget.

*A "Trade" is a company or individual (sometimes also referred to as a trade contractor, trade partner, construction trade, or subcontractor) providing labor to build any part of a project. Trades may also, in some situations, act as the supplier as well. For example a drywall trade may supply the drywall boards, drywall tape, corner bead, drywall tape compound, and fasteners, as well as the necessary labor to install the drywall.

Trades and Suppliers

Trades and suppliers embrace The Conflict-Free Home Remodeling Process because it shows respect for their time. In many cases where a typical project is "put out to bid," multiple remodelers and trade partners may be competing for the same project. While this may seem healthy, trade partners and suppliers know that without equal specifications as discussed in the previous sections of this book, their bid, or price, for their scope of the project may be completely skewed because one of their competitors may be looking at the project in a totally opposite and inferior manner.

Trade partners who work with remodelers using The Conflict-Free Home Remodeleing Process are more inclined to spend more time with the remodeler and the homeowner in an effort to help create a set of specifications and scope of work that most suits the homeowners' requirements. In turn, the content of their proposal will be more accurate and competitive because they will have had time to create a more meaningful proposal.

Remodeler

The remodeler benefits and wins with The Conflict-Free Home Remodeling Process because it allows him or her to build the project on paper first, eliminating an enormous number of potential mistakes that would otherwise occur in the field during the Construction phase. Knowing he or she is being paid for time spent in the Pre Construction phase, the remodeler feels comfortable spending the appropriate amount of time completing all of the steps necessary in this process.

Homeowner

The person who benefits the most from The Conflict-Free Home Remodeling Process is you - the most important person - the homeowner. Using the three steps outlined in the Pre Construction phase allows you to understand, in incremental steps, what your investment will be. This process takes your initial vision and through each step of the Pre Construction phase defines that vision, bringing you closer to the final actual cost. As you proceed along the Pre Construction path, you will have a firm understanding of what the real investment will be.

The majority of stress related to remodeling a home happens in the Construction phase. The vast majority of that stress is either eliminated or reduced when working with a remodeler who has adopted The Conflict-Free Home Remodeling Process. When the proper amount of time is spent prior to the actual start of construction, almost all of the potential points of contention found in the Construction phase are eliminated.

When a typical homeowner and remodeler enter into a relationship without an organized process, they are shooting from the hip, hoping to make the right decisions and hoping there is enough money to cover those decisions as they address them. One of the most frustrating things to witness is an unorganized remodeler without a process, forcing the homeowner to compromise his or her vision along the way, because the proper planning was not done to give the homeowner the information needed to make an educated decision.

A remodeler using The Conflict-Free Home Remodeling Process allows the homeowners to understand how much they will be investing for their project each step of the way, eliminating surprises. This process allows for a less stressful more peaceful path to fulfilling the homeowners' goals and dreams and avoids unnecessary compromises along the way.

Homeowner Success Story

Please let me share a residential home remodeling story that occurred recently. I prepared and presented a Feasibility Study for a 32-year construction veteran, Senior Vice President with Turner Construction, a company name you may know. This company builds hospitals, schools, and arenas – large commercial projects. I met with him and outlined everything I was going to do for a fee in order to formulate a preliminary budget for his remodeling ideas. After the Feasibility Study was performed and delivered, this veteran of the construction industry could not have been more complementary of the Conflict-Free Home Remodeling Process and the value it brought to him and his wife. A 32-year commercial construction veteran totally understood why he was paying a Pre Construction fee - he knew this information was necessary in order to determine if the scope of work and preliminary budget was right for him and his family – before investing any additional money for architectural plans.

Flexibility

Of course processes and procedures are the lines on the road and can occasionally be crossed, adjusted, or modified, based on the situation. The Conflict-Free Home Remodeling Process is designed to be as detailed or as simple as you choose. Interior remodels such as kitchens and bathrooms will get through the Pre Construction phase much quicker (some steps of the process can be consolidated or eliminated for a quicker turn-around) than a room addition or a whole house remodel.

We hope this book has helped you understand the information you need to plan successfully for a remodel or addition to your home or, what information you need to make the decision between remodeling or moving.

In either situation, hiring a remodeler who understands Up-Front Remodeling and The Conflict-Free Home Remodeling Process will be the first step in achieving your goals.

Continue Learning at REMODology®

Visit Today: *www.REMODology.com*

Homeowner Success Stories

The following homeowners used REMODology Remodeling Partners to provide The Conflict-Free Home Remodeling Process for their remodeling projects.

Read what they have to say:

Before the first nail was driven my remodeler met with me several times to gauge my needs, desires and budget to design a scope of work that met all my goals and became the roadmap for the project. The remodeler's team and I had mapped out how to achieve success before construction. During construction when there was a problem, as inevitably occurs in any remodeling project, because we had talked and planned extensively up-front documenting potential areas of concern and possible solutions, all problems were overcome with a minimum of delay and cost.

Upon completion of the project I was thoroughly thrilled with the result and the overall Conflict-Free experience. I sincerely believe the time taken in the beginning to discuss potential problems and areas of concern and tune in exactly to my goals really laid the foundation to what, ultimately, was an enjoyable experience. The workmanship and follow-through was excellent; the creative design suggested was exactly correct; and, in the end resulted in a "WOW" feeling.

Michael Abernethy
New York, New York

Up-Front Remodeling

Homeowner Success Stories

We interviewed a number of different companies and our remodeler was by far the most organized. We could tell they paid attention to detail. We had a smaller project completed on our house the year before, and that made us realize how important organization would be in doing a bigger project. In our initial meetings, everything was done on paper first. It assured us that things were not going to be missed.

Julie Jimenez
Orlando, Florida

After having a great experience completing a project with a remodeler that followed The Conflict-Free Home Remodeling Process I decided to do my next project with a remodeler that was less expensive and recommended by friends. This second remodeling project taught me the value of spending time and money to plan and organize at the beginning makes a huge difference during construction.

Organizing and planning up-front, and knowing each step made the construction phase easy. My second remodeling experience was very frustrating due to the fact I was always in the dark: there wasn't a checklist to follow; I never knew when the crews would be working; there was strife amongst subcontractors; the company I hired could never give me the dates they needed specific materials from me. With the company that provided Conflict-Free remodeling, they could always show me what step we were at during construction and I knew 2 to 3 weeks ahead of time what the next step of the project would be.

The results are night and day. Using a remodeling company that did not provide Pre Construction services resulted in 7 months of frustration and unforeseen costs I had to pay since the project was not completed on time. I feel in the end after comparing the two remodelers, using the remodeler that provided the Conflict Free Process saved me time and created less stress.

Pam Oldham
Orlando, Florida

Glossary

Allowance

This term refers to an arbitrary dollar amount assigned to a particular item not yet selected by the homeowner in the Pre Construction phase of The Conflict-Free Home Remodeling Process. Depending on the actual amount spent on a particular allowance item, the homeowner will pay an additional amount (if the item costs more than the allowance) or will be given a credit (if the item costs less than the allowance).

Architect

An architect is an individual who designs homes or buildings and, in some cases, participates in overseeing the construction of the home or building designed. An architect is someone who has completed four years of college education and received a Bachelor of Arts or Bachelor of Science degree in Architectural Studies. Additionally, an architect who goes on to earn a Master of Architecture degree is qualified to become a licensed architect. Some universities offer a 5-year program called a Bachelor of Architecture, also qualifying for licensure. To acquire licensure an architect must pass an exam in the particular state in which he or she wishes to be licensed.

Architectural Review Board

An architectural review board is also referred to as an ARB or DRC (Design Review Committee). ARBs are usually found where there is an organized homeowners' association. This board or committee is a group of individuals usually comprised of home building professionals such as a custom home builder, remodeler, or architect, as well as homeowners living in the neighborhood. The purpose of the ARB is to review proposed plans for additions or modifications to the exterior of the home to assure they harmonize with the existing architecture of the home and character of the neighborhood as outlined (typically) in written design guidelines.

Bid Conference

The bid conference is held at the homeowner's home – the location of the remodeling project. All key trades and suppliers are invited to the bid conference to review the existing as-built conditions as well as the proposed plans.

Budget

The budget in the Feasibility Study step of The Conflict-Free Home Remodeling Process is a forecast of what the cost of the project may be, based on a preliminary scope of work and allowances. In the Design Review step, the budget represents a more defined cost for the project. In the Final Plans & Specifications step, the budget is the final cost of the project, assuming there are no addendums or cost differential to any allowances.

Building permit

A building permit is generally required in most municipalities when performing interior or exterior work to an existing home. The proposed scope of work is documented on a plan and submitted to the municipal building department for review. Upon approval of the plan, the building improvements can begin.

CAD

Computer aided design or computer aided drafting.

Casing

Decorative, composite or other, trim installed around the two vertical sides and top horizontal side of a door or installed around the two vertical sides and top horizontal side of a window. In the absence of a window sill, casing is sometimes installed on the bottom horizontal side of a window.

Glossary

Conceptual plan

A hand or CAD-drawn line sketch of the floor plan and sometimes elevations giving an abstract or generic idea of what the improvements will look like. Conceptual plans are used during the Feasibility Study step of The Remodeling Process.

Construction drawings

The construction drawings, also called working drawings or construction plans, are the combination of the architects', engineers', and designers' plans (the plans are the large pieces of paper measuring approximately 36" wide x 24" high – sometimes bigger or smaller) from the disciplines who have participated in developing the technical aspects of the project. The construction drawings show sufficient technical detail so that whatever is shown can be built.

Design

Design is the plans for the construction of an addition or remodel. The plans include the architectural construction drawings and interior designer's drawings–any document conveying information as to what the project will look like visually.

Design build

Design build is a concept whereby one entity (the remodeler) or collectively two or more entities (remodeler and architect) combine services to design and build a project. This process: 1) Allows the design team to interact with the construction team during development of the project, and 2) Streamlines the process for the client.

Diffusers

A rectangular, square or round outlet vent attached to the HVAC ductwork to allow the supply of heated or cooled air to be distributed into a given space. Most diffusers are adjustable, allowing the user to adjust the volume of flow through the diffuser. Diffusers are sometimes referred to as registers.

Ducts

Ducts are passageways used for the movement of air through a heating, ventilating, and air conditioning (HVAC) system. Typical residential ducts are made of hard insulated fiberglass duct board cut to a specific required size or a round flexible plastic tube with a layer of insulation and metal wire for support.

Elevations

Elevations refer to two-dimensional graphic representations of vertical elements of the interior or exterior of a project. An exterior elevation may show what the exterior of a home will look like from the ground up to the top of the roof, including the windows and doors, wall surface, fascia, and roofing material. An interior elevation may show a particular architectural feature such as the kitchen cabinet elevation or fireplace facade elevation.

Engineer

Engineer refers primarily to a structural engineer. A structural engineer is a licensed professional who reviews any plan requiring work to the structure, including but not limited to the building foundation, floor or roof trusses, or wall sections. The structural engineer assures the proper sizing and placement of those components.

Glossary

Engineer (continued)

The term engineer may also refer to a civil, mechanical, electrical, or plumbing engineer; however, typically these engineers are not required or needed for most residential construction projects.

Final agreement

The final agreement is a collection of documents prepared in the Pre Construction phase and used to convey the project details to every person involved in the Construction phase. The components of the final agreement include: 1) Final Plans, 2) Final Specifications, 3) Final Product Selections, 4) Final Budget, 5) Allowance Schedule, 6) Payment Schedule, and 7) General Conditions.

Floor plan

A line drawing illustrating the horizontal outline (length and width) of a certain floor space or spaces; i.e. the whole house floor plan or the master bedroom floor plan.

General Conditions

General Conditions are the business side of the final construction agreement and apply to the legal, business and conflict resolution side of The Conflict-Free Home Remodeling Process. General Conditions touch on a number of subjects that quite possibly may come up during the Construction phase. General Conditions are designed to help each party know what he or she is or is not responsible for and are essentially the governing rules and regulations between the homeowner and the remodeler.

Green building

Green building (also known as green construction or sustainable building) is the practice of creating structures and using processes that are environmentally responsible and resource-efficient throughout a building's life-cycle: from siting to design, construction, operation, maintenance, remodeling, and deconstruction.

Impervious coverage

Also referred to as impervious lot coverage, this indicator means the property has a maximum permitted impervious coverage limit (measured by percentage). Impervious means resistant to movement of water, i.e., water cannot percolate through the surface of the object. Impervious coverage typically includes all building areas at ground level, driveways, sidewalks, and patios.

Interior Decorator

An interior decorator is not required to have completed any formal education in order to call him/herself an interior decorator. Interior decorators are most helpful in specifying and selecting the products needed in an addition or remodel (i.e., plumbing fixtures, electrical fixtures, tile, cabinets, countertops, etc.) and color selections for the products to be installed in the project.

Interior Designer

An interior designer is one who has completed a bachelor's degree in interior design and who is qualified to sit for and pass a state exam in order to be called a licensed interior designer. Not all states require interior designers to be licensed, nor do they all offer licensing exams.

Living space

Living space, as opposed to space "under roof," which encompasses all spaces with a roof above, pertains only those spaces that are heated and cooled.

Glossary

Load bearing

Load bearing refers to a wall or any part of the building structure that carries a structural load on top of it. Exterior walls are load bearing because they carry the weight of a second floor or the weight of a roof truss on top. Some interior walls may be load bearing if they have a second floor truss resting on top, or a section of a long spanning roof truss bearing on the wall or beam.

Moulding (Molding)

Decorative wood, stone or composite material (sometimes referred to as trim) used on the interior or exterior of the home for ornamentation or finishing.

Municipality

A municipality is a local governing body including but not limited to city, town, county, parish or township.

Notice of commencement

In many states a notice of commencement is required to inform interested third parties who the homeowner and lender (if applicable) are. Prior to the start of construction (in some cases, before the first inspection) a notice of commencement is required to be filed with the appropriate local municipal authority – usually the clerk of courts.

Plans

Plans, also called construction drawings, are the combination of the architect's, engineers' and designers' drawings (the plans are the large pieces of paper measuring approximately 36" wide x 24" high – sometimes bigger or smaller) from the disciplines who have participated in developing the technical aspects of the project.

Preliminary budget

The preliminary budget is arrived at as a result of the Feasibility Study. The preliminary budget is a forecast of what the cost of the project may be, based on a preliminary scope of work and allowances.

Preliminary plan

The preliminary plan is developed during the Design Review step of the Pre Construction phase and is a hand or CAD-drawn line sketch of the floor plan and exterior elevations, giving a more detailed idea of what the improvements will look like. The preliminary plan is more refined than the conceptual plan developed for the Feasibility Study step of The Conflict-Free Home Remodeling Process.

Product selections

Product selections are the finish products used for the project requiring approval by the homeowner prior to the purchase and installation of each product. Product selections include but are not limited to floor covering, cabinets, counter tops, appliances, hardware, plumbing fixtures, electrical fixtures, and paint colors. Product selections are either selected by the homeowner or with the assistance of an interior designer or decorator.

Residential Designer

The term residential designer means an individual who designs new custom homes, remodels, or additions to existing residential dwellings. Residential designers require no formal education or training in the field of residential design or architecture. Anyone can call himself/herself a residential designer. For a residential designer to be distinguished above his or her peers and advance to another level, the American Institute of Building Design (AIBD), offers the resources to do so.

Glossary

Residential Designer (continued)

Most AIBD residential designers strive to educate themselves in a manner that produces the most technically correct and architecturally pleasing custom homes, remodels, and additions.

Scope of work

Scope of work is a descriptive outline of the work to take place, for example:
- a) Master bedroom addition with a new bathroom including two sinks, a tub, and a shower.
- b) New porch off of the master bedroom addition.
- c) Convert the existing master bedroom, closet and bathroom into a den.
- d) Re-roof the entire home.
- e) Re-paint the entire exterior of the home.

Setback

A local code or ordinance specifying the minimum distance that a building may be located in relation to the street or property line.

Superintendent

A construction superintendent is responsible for scheduling trades and suppliers to the project and is the point of contact with the homeowner during the Construction phase. In some cases, the superintendent has two or three or more projects he or she is responsible for at the same time. Given the fact that the superintendent has more than one project to oversee; he or she cannot spend eight hours a day at any one project. His or her job is to stop by the project, typically once or twice a day, to inspect the work, make sure it is confirming to the Final Plans & Specifications agreed to, answer any questions the workers may have, and field phone calls as they come in. Typically, the superintendent does not perform any manual labor.

Supplier

Any company (sometimes also referred to as a vendor), retail or wholesale, providing raw or finished materials or equipment for the project.

Survey

- Boundary survey - A boundary survey is a document outlining the boundaries of a parcel of land and including the dimensions of each of those boundaries.
- Boundary survey with improvements - A boundary survey with improvements includes all horizontal (sidewalks and driveways) and vertical (buildings) improvements to the property, including the dimensions.
- Topographical survey - A topographical survey indicates the contour of the land typically in 1'0" increments.
- Foundation survey – Locates the outline of a new building foundation after it has been constructed.

Trade

A company or individual (sometimes also referred to as a trade contractor, trade partner, construction trade, or subcontractor) providing labor to build any part of a project. Trades may also, in some situations, act as the supplier as well. For example a drywall trade may supply the drywall boards, drywall tape, corner bead, drywall tape compound, and fasteners, as well as the necessary labor to install the drywall.

Glossary

Truss - A truss can be a roof truss or a floor truss and is usually prefabricated at a remote location and delivered by truck to the project site.

Roof Truss - A roof truss is comprised of several pieces of (typically) wood to form a reinforced triangle shape and create two exterior planes (the roof) and one interior plane (the ceiling) of a structure.

Floor Truss - A floor truss is comprised of several pieces of (typically) wood to form an elongated rectangle with the top and bottom edges (chords) parallel to one another and reinforcing supports placed at an angle to the top and bottom chords.

Under roof

Under roof pertains to any room or part of the home with a roof over its floor surface. Garages, covered entries, covered porches or lanais, basements, and living space are all considered under roof.

Wall section

A wall section is a cut-through of a particular vertical wall of the home drawn by the architect. The wall section can be an interior or exterior wall. The wall section allows the remodeler, trades, and suppliers to determine how the wall will be constructed and what materials will be used.

START THE PROCESS ON YOUR OWN – PURCHASE THE BOOK

Conflict-Free Home Remodeling

The Home Remodeling Process Builds Harmony

▶ Purchase the book Conflict-Free Home Remodeling to learn all the details of how The Home Remodeling Process builds harmony between your budget and design, your family and the construction crews, your savings and unnecessary changes.

▶ Using a fictitious project, this step-by-step book takes you through the three most important steps of the Pre Construction phase in great detail.

▶ The Pre Construction phase prepares you each step of the way as you plan your project and most importantly, helps you arrive at a realistic budget for the cost of your remodeling project before construction.

▶ Prior to starting the actual Construction phase of The Conflict-Free Home Remodeling Process you will know exactly what you will be getting, how much it will cost plus how to keep your family and assets safe.

Purchase Your Book at www.REMODology.com

Begin Getting Answers for Your Specific Remodeling Project's Details and Costs

or

START PLANNING YOUR REMODELING PROJECT TODAY! FIND A REMODELER WHO PROVIDES

The Conflict-Free Home Remodeling Process

▶ Contact the right remodeler at REMODology.com. Find a remodeler who will become your partner to help you meet your goals by guiding you through the Conflict-Free Home Remodeling Process.

View Remodeling Partner profiles and company web sites at REMODology.com

Other titles for the homeowner from the REMODology® series and Stephen Gidus:

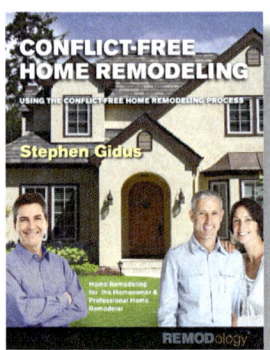

Conflict-Free Home Remodeling
Using the Conflict-Free Home Remodeling Process

This book is the centerpiece of REMODology. If you are thinking about a home addition or remodeling project, you may be about to invest what might be the largest amount of money you have ever invested in anything – except for the purchase of your home. The premise behind this book is: spending time researching and preparing before you start your remodeling project will lead to a greater return on your investment and a much more successful completion of your vision for your home.

Learn how applying The Conflict-Free Home Remodeling Process builds harmony between:

- **Your budget and the design** - This highly practical resource will show you a step-by-step process to identify your wants and needs, to determine if your remodeling dream is feasible.
- **Your family and the construction crews** - Use this book to help guide you in making sure the right tasks are being considered for your family's lifestyle needs before construction crews begin work.
- **Your savings and unnecessary changes** - Learn how building on paper first will save you time and money by avoiding unnecessary changes.

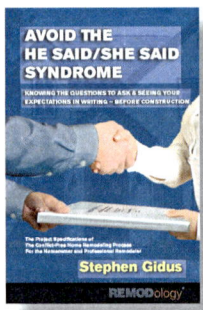

Avoid the He Said/She Said Syndrome
Knowing the Questions to Ask & Seeing Your Expectations in Writing – Before Construction

Many hours of discussion will take place in the planning phase of a home remodeling project. Potentially, hundreds of options will be presented, examined, reviewed, and deliberated. The project specifications are all of the final decisions and promises in writing, to be agreed on before the start of construction. Make sure you get what you want by discussing every possible item up-front and then have it documented into a final set of project specifications specifically for your home remodeling project. Use the outlined specifications in this book as talking points with your remodeler. *Avoid the He Said/She Said Syndrome* helps facilitate discussion about all of the possible choices you have for your remodeling project.

Peaceful Home Remodeling
Avoid Litigation with Your Home Remodeler

Nothing is more pleasing to a homeowner than no surprises during construction. Nothing is more rewarding to a home remodeler than a happy homeowner after a project is completed. Successful and peaceful relationships between remodelers and homeowners do not happen by chance. They are deliberate. Peaceful relationships happen because the home remodeler sets homeowner expectations up-front before the start of construction – and he or she documents those expectations. Every potential situation that can occur during a home remodeling project is addressed in this book in order to facilitate intelligent discussion with your remodeler before starting construction.

REMODology®

Building Harmony and Win-Win Relationships
Between Homeowners and Remodelers

WA WORD ASSOCIATION
PUBLISHERS

643.7 G453

Gidus, Stephen
Up-front remodeling : avoid
the home remodeling letdown
by knowing all details and
costs before construction
Ring ADU CIRC
04/12

Friends of the
Houston Public Library